MYTHS
OF THE
MIDDLE AGES

MYTHS OF THE MIDDLE AGES

Sabine Baring-Gould
Edited by John Matthews

Foreword by Cyril Tawney

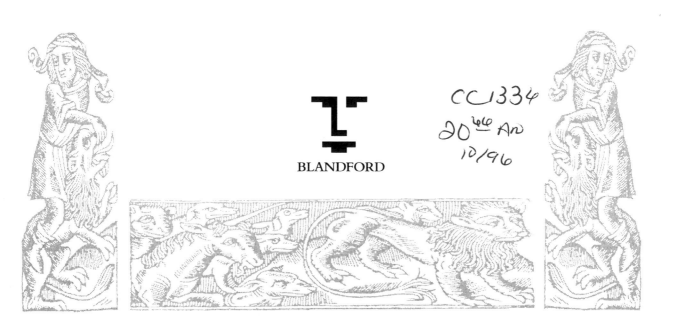

BLANDFORD

First published in the UK 1996 by Blandford
A Cassell Imprint

Cassell Plc
Wellington House
125 Strand
London WC2R 0BB

Distributed in the United States by Sterling Publishing Co., Inc.
387 Park Avenue South, New York, NY 10016-8810

Distributed in Australia by Capricorn Link (Australia) Pty Ltd
2/13 Carrington Road, Castle Hill, NSW 2154

**A Cataloguing-in-Publication Data entry for this title is
available from the British Library**

ISBN 0–7137–2607–5

Colour illustrations by Peter Komarnyckyj
Typeset by Keystroke, Jacaranda Lodge, Wightwick Bank, Wolverhampton
Printed and bound in Spain by Bookprint

Contents

Foreword

An Appreciation of the Life and Work of
the Reverend Sabine Baring-Gould
by Cyril Tawney

ONE EVENING in the mid-1960s, a television magazine programme to which I was a regular contributor included a special feature on the Reverend Sabine Baring-Gould. In the best TV tradition, instead of simply *telling* viewers how many books this astonishing man had written, all, or very nearly all, were brought into the studio. The stack was as high as an average garden wall and stretched almost the entire length of the studio. It was an imposing sight and must have produced the maximum visual impact.

Baring-Gould's grandson and biographer, the Rev. Bickford Dickinson, reminds us that 'at one time he had listed under his name in the catalogue of the British Museum Library more books than any other English author, so many indeed that like other prolific authors he was unjustly suspected of employing "ghosts"'.

This fact would be impressive enough, but the range of his work is equally amazing, and was evidently likely to engender disbelief as much as astonishment. I once came across an issue of a contemporary antiquarian journal in which the editor was having to assure a lady reader that the author of a recent scholarly article was indeed the same 'S. Baring-Gould' who had written the string of romantic novels to which she had become so addicted. Just as noteworthy as his output, though purely incidental, is that fact that it was his custom to do all this writing in longhand, standing at a lectern.

My personal introduction to Baring-Gould's work – apart, that is, from knowing he was the author of the hymn 'Onward Christian Soldiers' – came through his collection of folk-songs from Devon and Cornwall. In the late 1950s I settled in Plymouth as a full-time practitioner of English traditional songs, with a particular interest in those from the South and West. I soon found myself making a close study of Baring-Gould's body of material, especially his unpublished manuscripts deposited in Plymouth Public Library. Until recently, it was assumed that these, together with the published collections, constituted the entire surviving record of Baring-Gould's song-collecting campaign. I am delighted to say that, at the moment of writing, a whole new treasure trove of manuscripts containing an even greater number of songs has been discovered which should keep folk-song scholars busy for years to come.

Baring-Gould was an antiquarian by instinct and, as with his song-collecting, much of his work in this field was inspired by an anxiety that certain things of value were dying out and in need of rescue and preservation. We can sympathize more with this attitude when the extraordinary dimensions of his life are realized. In historical terms alone, its span was of a kind allotted to few people. Having been born and raised among veterans of Trafalgar and Waterloo, in an age when the fastest mode of travel was the horse, he died surrounded by survivors of the Battles of Jutland and the Somme in the First World War, a bare three years before Lindbergh flew solo across the Atlantic.

Also, passionate Englishman though Baring-Gould was, his upbringing – one of almost perpetual European touring with his parents – gave him a linguistic facility and a continental overview which would be the envy of any British diplomat today. Add to this background a knowledge of printed sources second to none, plus a very accessible prose style, and his success as a popularizer and educator was almost guaranteed.

So much is heard nowadays about conserving 'this' and protecting 'that', yet hardly a whisper of concern is uttered by these same people about the menacing effect of modern existence upon our priceless oral traditions. Does their zeal stop short of something that cannot be quantified or measured? Particularly in the field of folklore, of which medieval mythology is a substantial part, any revival of Sabine Baring-Gould's work is to be warmly welcomed.

A Dream of the Middle Ages

THE MIDDLE AGES has been called a credulous age, an age coloured by a superstitious belief in the most unlikely and bizarre things. Certainly travellers' tales like those collected in the fourteenth-century best-seller *The Travels of Sir John Mandeville*, which could include a description such as the following, give one pause for thought:

> In this wilderness are many wild men with horns on their heads: they dwell in the woods and speak not, only grunting like pigs. And in some woods in that land are wild dogs that will never come near to man, any more than foxes do in this country. There are birds, too, that of their own nature speak and call out to men who are crossing the desert, speaking as clearly as if they were men. These birds have large tongues and five claws on each foot. There are others that have only three claws on each foot, and they do not speak so well or clearly. These birds are called parrots . . . [1]

In much the same way theological arguments centring around the date of Creation, the sex of angels and the number of these divine beings that it was possible to stand upon the head of a pin, may lead one to suppose that there was a more than credulous desire to believe in the most extraordinary 'facts'.

Yet it must also be said that we are hardly less inclined to believe in odd or questionable things today – be they UFOs, monsters, or the ability of science to create a perfect world. The number of books and tabloid newspapers read avidly by people all over the world – and apparently believed by a larger number – show this to be true.

The fact of the matter is that we are a credulous species, continually seeking to transcend the limiting view of the world presented to us by our five senses and to find new dimensions of the extraordinary and the astounding. This has led, within the last twenty-odd years, to a renewal of interest in magic, myth, and disciplines once considered the preserve of ancient tribal societies, such as shamanism, divination, and reincarnation.

In the Middle Ages, of course, such things would have been considered heretical and would, in all likelihood, have earned their practitioners a short walk to the stake. But there were those who successfully practised the 'forbidden arts' and much of their knowledge became encoded in the popular literature of the time. Thus, when we read of the Quest for the Grail we are hearing far more than a simple story; and when the subject turns to Prester John, the Terrestrial Paradise, or the Mountain of Venus (all of which receive due attention in this collection), we are witnessing not just idle curiosity but a far deeper, spiritual longing which is expressed in these stories of transcendent events.

The people of the Middle Ages believed in what the author of this book calls these 'curious myths', not with a slavish literalness, but with a sensitivity to a greater reality than that offered by the five senses. In this they reflect a certain innocence which is like that of a child rather than a credulous adult. There is a sense of newness, of childlike faith in wonders, which comes through these stories, the same raw spirit which created them in the first place.

Not that they were not sophisticated. Many of the medieval masterpieces, such as Sir Thomas Malory's *Mort D'Arthur*[2] or Wolfram von Eschenbach's *Parzival*,[3] were literary masterpieces, displaying a wide range of psychological insight as well as a deep and lasting appreciation of the living world – whether it was filled with curiosities or not.

Sabine Baring-Gould was aware of this when he compiled the wide-ranging series of essays from which a selection is included here. He goes to the widest possible range of sources, treating them for the most part with the same objectivity as he might have viewed an account of a contemporary traveller, or a writer of 'true' ghost stories. It is this objectivity which gives the collection presented here its remarkable power – a power which has scarcely diminished since the collection was first published in 1868.

The author himself was a man of astonishingly wide knowledge and ability. He wrote something in the region of two hundred books, including fifty novels (all now forgotten), biographies, essays, poetry, travel books, collections of myths and folklore, and numerous religious works. As well as being best remembered as the author of the words to the well-known hymn 'Onward Christian Soldiers' and for giving the world the folk-song 'Uncle Tom Cobley', it is as a writer and avid collector of rare and out-of-the-way information that he also deserves to be known.

Born in 1834 into a well-to-do family, Gould was educated at King's College School in London and later at Clare College, Cambridge. Ordained in 1864, he became the curate of Horbury Brig in West Yorkshire. There he met his future wife Grace Taylor, a mill girl who, in a notable Victorian romance, he wooed and married and who subsequently bore him an astonishing sixteen children. It was said indeed that Gould could not himself ever quite recall how many offspring he had, and the story is told that at a children's Christmas party one year he spied a child in a pretty dress descending the stairs. Looming over her in his black clothes he asked kindly: 'Whose little girl are you, my dear?' to which the child, bursting into tears, replied: 'I'm yours, Daddy.'

In 1867 Gould moved from Horbury to the parish of Dalton in the East Riding of Yorkshire. There he remained until 1871 when he moved to East Mersea on the Essex coast. A year later his father died and he inherited the family estate at Lew Trenchard in Devon. He moved there in 1881 and was installed as the incumbent of the local church. Gould was to remain in the village until his death in 1924, one of the last 'squarsons' or squire-parsons holding both the office of squire and that of rector within the parish.

During all this time, no matter where he was, Gould wrote. Words quite literally poured from his pen, as he followed a strict rule of writing at least a single chapter every day, working early in the morning and completing his daily stint before turning his attention to his duties as squire and parson.

One of his biographers, W. E. Purcell, has written of Gould:

> He was not an orator; he was not an exact scholar. As antiquary and archaeologist inaccurate, as writer careless of the seam of genius noticed by Swinburne and Barrie, he yet had, and still has, fascination of a kind never perhaps to be repeated.[4]

Once settled at Lew Trenchard, Gould began a wide-ranging exploration of the archaeology of Devon, a subject in which he had been interested since his schooldays. Over the next few years he published a number of articles in the Transactions of the Devonshire Association. They include 'A Lost Lake', 'Some Devon Monoliths', and 'The Exploration of Grimspound'. On the whole, however, Gould was not a good archaeologist, preferring to make extravagant guesses and measure distances by pace rather than the careful millimetres of current archaeological science. His approach merely reflects yet again a strong fascination with the past and its mysteries.

Of any deeper meaning inherent in these mysteries he remained personally detached, despite, or perhaps because of, an incident in his own childhood. It seems that while travelling in Europe with his family in 1837 Gould himself saw 'a little crowd of imps or dwarfs surrounding the carriage, some running along beside the horses, some jumping upon their backs. One was astride behind the post-boy. They were dressed in brown, with puce breeches, and wore little scarlet caps . . . ' Though his father at once insisted he ride inside the coach and forbade him to mention the subject again, it seems likely that Gould never forgot the incident, and that it may well have influenced his later preoccupation with the otherworldly.

Sabine Baring-Gould's literary life began with the publication, in 1857, of *The Path of the Just*, a devotional book reflecting on death and eternity. This was followed, after a trip to Iceland, by *Iceland, Its Scenes and Sagas* in 1863, then by *Post-Medieval Preachers* and *The Book of Were-Wolves*. After his ordination in 1864 he wrote his first novel, *Through Flood and Flame*. Then came a series of collections of folklore and faery-tales, more travel books and the first of numerous volumes of essays, sermons and biographies, including one of another West Country eccentric and parson, Robert Stephen Hawker, best remembered today for his odd poem 'The Quest of the Sangreal'.

But Gould's arguably most important work was in the collection of folk-songs in his native Devon and neigbouring Cornwall. For almost fifteen years he laboured to assemble, transcribe and, finally, to publish, his *Songs of the West* (1895), containing a huge body of folk-songs sung by the people of Devon and Cornwall. When it appeared in book form it earned its author some success – although as a Victorian, and a parson at that, the fact that Gould had systematically bowdlerized the bawdy songs of the stone-masons, farmworkers and thatchers subsequently damaged his reputation as a collector of folk-songs. With all the care of many such Victorian scholars, Gould deposited the original versions of the songs – altogether 202 in number – in the Plymouth City Library, where they may still be seen today. These are meticulously copied out, in full, with music, and are a lasting testament to Gould's care and devotion to the subject.

His other writings are of less value, however. The novels are of their time and possess none of the finesse of Thomas Hardy or Mary Webb, though there are some powerful tales among them, notably *The Red Spider* of 1887, *The Pennycomequicks* (1889) and *The Broom Squire* – for some time Gould's most popular book – published in 1896. All of the books are filled with a rich gallery of 'country' characters and coloured by a deep feeling for the natural world, which Gould described with passion and delight, as in the following passage from *In Dewisland* (1904):

> In the summertime, when the sun shines, the sea in the Channel is of the clearest crystal green, just touched here and there with plumes of silver. Contrasting with this translucent green are the red and purple cliffs, and the glorious mantle of crimson heather, brocaded with the gold of the gorse, that the island wraps around it.

In some ways, Gould led a double life: on the one hand, he was the kindly, austere country parson; on the other, the successful man of letters. Indeed, so great was the seeming distance between the two sides of his character that on one occasion a lady, on being introduced to him, asked: 'Are you the good Mr Baring-Gould who writes such beautiful sermons, or the other Mr Baring-Gould who writes novels?'

Let the best of his biographers, W. E. Purcell, sum him up:

> His was the genius of prodigality . . . The undisturbed years, succeeding each other like the placid ticking of a clock on a weekday afternoon in some country church, providing the solid framework in which so amazingly individual, so diffuse a genius, could flower . . . There is Sabine the devout . . . There is Sabine the hagiographer . . . There is the Baedeker Sabine, producing glorified guide books; the journalist Sabine, facile, quick-working, delighting in the curious: ghouls, were-wolves, the origin of headless horses as premonitions of death. The biographer Sabine, building, in *Cornish Characters* and its companion for Devon, a monument to those worthies and eccentrics who once so richly adorned local life.[5]

To this impressive list Purcell adds the Baring-Gould of the Catholic Revival, the Gould whose strongly held belief stares out from so many of the pages of the essays gathered together in this book. A man of faith who yet desired to see some way beyond the ordinary and who sought, in his writings, to delve deeper into the odd corners of the world, as represented here by these 'curious myths'.

Gould was a collector of strange lore for most of his life. The first volume of *Curious Myths* appeared in 1866 and was followed by a second collection two years later. The books were sufficiently popular to warrant republication in a single volume in 1869 – the source of this present selection. In the same year his *Curiosities of Ancient Times* appeared and in 1874 two other volumes, *Yorkshire Oddities* and *Strange Events*, which were later reissued as *Historical Oddities*, an almost Fortean collection of odd things. Gould wrote in the introduction to the latter book:

> An antiquary lights upon many a curiosity whilst overhauling the dusty tomes of ancient writers. This little book is a small museum in which I have preserved some of the quaintest relics which have attracted me during my labour.

It would make a fitting epigraph to the current collection.

In making a selection from the original twenty-four essays in the one-volume edition of Gould's *Curious Myths* I have tried to pick those which have the most intrinsic merits and the most to say to a contemporary readership. Beyond this I have edited them very lightly, letting Gould's sometimes outlandish opinions stand as part of the man, and refraining from changing any of his occasionally odd punctuation. Copies of the original book still turn up occasionally in second-hand bookshops, and I would recommend those who enjoyed the present selection to seek out one of these. Several other essays are worth re-reading, especially those on William Tell, St George, St Patrick's Purgatory and the Piper of Hameln.

JOHN MATTHEWS
Oxford

[1] *The Travels of Sir John Mandeville*, translated by C. W. R. D. Moseley (Harmondsworth: Penguin Books, 1983).
[2] Sir Thomas Malory, *Le Morte D'Arthur* (New York: University Books, 1962).
[3] Wolfram von Eschenbach, *Parzival*, translated by T. Hatto (Harmondsworth: Penguin Books, 1968).
[4] W. E. Purcell, *Onward Christian Soldier: A Life of Sabine Baring-Gould* (London: Longmans, Green, 1957).
[5] Purcell, *Onward Christian Soldier*.

CHAPTER 1

Prester John

THE STORY of a priestly king ruling over a Christian empire in the Far East has exerted a powerful fascination over the minds of Western writers and historians since rumours of the existence of such a figure first found their way into popular conciousness from the report of Otto of Freising around 1145. This report, which was itself at least of second-hand origin, is now generally accepted to be a garbled version of an actual historical event – the defeat of the Seljuk Sultan Sanjar by the Quara Khitai somewhere on the Quatvan Steppe near Samarkand in the year 1141. In the four intervening years the story had grown until it became the fantastic account which Otto claimed to have heard from the lips of Bishop Hugh of Jabala while travelling in the Lebanon.

From here the story grew, drawing upon biblical sources, Hebrew legends and travellers' tall tales. Then, in approximately 1165, a letter purporting to be from 'John, Priest by the Almighty power of God . . . King of Kings, and Lord of Lords . . .' etc. was sent to various crowned heads of the Western world and to Pope Alexander III. It contained a long and fantastic account of the lands ruled over by the 'Priest-King'. The letter exists in a number of versions, and several languages, including Latin, Hebrew, Teutonic and Slavonic. Most versions are similar enough to have derived from a common source, though it is impossible to say with any certainty which is the earliest.

The language of the letter and its imagery make it clear that the author (or authors) was drawing upon a wide range of materials, centring around the existence of a Terrestrial Paradise (see also Chapter 7) with a strongly biblical tone. To this have been added details borrowed liberally from the accounts of medieval travellers such as Marco Polo and 'Sir John Mandeville' – though none are so exact as to include a precise textual source.

9

Recent scholarship has suggested a number of possible contenders for the origin of Prester John, including the Unk-Khan mentioned by Gould, as well as Chingis-Khan and the Negus of Ethiopia. (Any are possible since the name Prester John probably means 'the priest of John,' i.e., St John the Evangelist.) Gould's suggestion that the source of the belief in a Christian kingdom in the East derives from the establishment of the Nestorian Church in parts of India and Ethiopia seems the most believable today.

It has often been maintained that the letter, with its implication of the existence of a Christian ally 'behind the lines' of the Islamic kingdoms, was intended to act as a palliative to the beleaguered West. However, the evidence of several full translations (see below) suggests that it was intended as much to be an attack on the popes and the Church of Rome – perhaps by the exiled Nestorians.

Another aspect of the Prester John tradition not mentioned by Gould is his appearance in the genealogy of the Grail kings. In Wolfram von Eschenbach's twelfth-century poem *Parzival* he is the son of the Grail hero's brother Feirefiz and his lady Repanse de Schoy – thus making him cousin to King Arthur. In the medieval Dutch *Lancelot* he appears as the son of Perceval himself. Modern esoteric tradition has appointed him guardian of the Grail for the twentieth century. As a semi-fictitious figure whose origins may well be forever clouded, Prester John continues to live on tenaciously in Western literature.

*   *   *

ABOUT the middle of the twelfth century, a rumour circulated through Europe that there reigned in Asia a powerful Christian Emperor, Presbyter Johannes. In a bloody fight he had broken the power of the Mussulmans, and was ready to come to the assistance of the Crusaders. Great was the exultation in Europe, for of late the news from the East had been gloomy and depressing, the power of the infidel had increased, overwhelming masses of men had been brought into the field against the chivalry of Christendom, and it was felt that the cross must yield before the odious crescent.

The news of the success of the Priest-King opened a door of hope to the desponding Christian world. Pope Alexander III determined at once to effect a union with this mysterious personage, and on the 27th of September, 1177, wrote him a letter, which he entrusted to his physician, Philip, to deliver in person.

Philip started on his embassy, but never returned. The conquests of Tschengis-Khan again attracted the eyes of Christian Europe to the East. The Mongol hordes were rushing in upon the West with devastating ferocity; Russia, Poland, Hungary, and the Eastern provinces of Germany, had succumbed, or suffered grievously; and the fears of other nations were roused lest they too should taste the misery of a Mongolian invasion It was Gog and Magog come to slaughter, and the times of Antichrist were dawning. But the battle of Liegnitz stayed them in their onward career, and Europe was saved.

Pope Innocent IV determined to convert these wild hordes of barbarians, and subject them to the cross of Christ; he therefore sent among them a number of

Dominican and Franciscan missioners, and embassies of peace passed between the Pope, the King of France, and the Mogul Khan.

The result of these communications with the East was that the travellers learned how false were the prevalent notions of a mighty Christian empire existing in central Asia. Vulgar superstition or conviction is not, however, to be upset by evidence, and the locality of the monarchy was merely transferred by the people to Africa, and they fixed upon Abyssinia, with a show of truth, as the seat of the famous Priest-King. However, still some doubted. John de Plano-Carpini and Marco Polo, though they acknowledged the existence of a Christian monarch in Abyssinia, yet stoutly maintained as well that the Prester John of popular belief reigned in splendour somewhere in the dim Orient.

But before proceeding with the history of this strange fable, it will be well to extract the different accounts given of the Priest-King and his realm by early writers; and we shall then be better able to judge of the influence the myth obtained in Europe.

Otto of Freisingen is the first author to mention the monarchy of Prester John, with whom we are acquainted. Otto wrote a chronicle up to the date 1156, and he relates that in 1145 the Catholic Bishop of Cabala visited Europe to lay certain complaints before the Pope. He mentioned the fall of Edessa, and also 'he stated that a few years ago a certain King and Priest called John, who lives on the further side of Persia and Armenia in the remote East, and who, with all his people, were Christians, though belonging to the Nestorian Church, had overcome the royal brothers Samiardi, kings of the Medes and Persians, and had captured Ecbatana, their capital and residence. The said kings had met with their Persian, Median, and Assyrian troops, and had fought for three consecutive days, each side having determined to die rather than take to flight. Prester John, for so they are wont to call him, at length routed the Persians, and after a bloody battle, remained victorious. After which victory the said John was hastening to the assistance of the Church at Jerusalem, but his host, on reaching the Tigris, was hindered from passing through a deficiency in boats, and he directed his march North, since he had heard that the river was there covered with ice. In that place he had waited many years, expecting severe cold, but the winters having proved unpropitious, and the severity of the climate having carried off many soldiers, he had been forced to retreat to his own land. This king belongs to the family of the Magi, mentioned in the Gospel, and he rules over the very people formerly governed by the Magi; moreover, his fame and his wealth is so great, that he uses an emerald sceptre only.

'Excited by the example of his ancestors, who came to worship Christ in His cradle, he had proposed to go to Jerusalem, but had been impeded by the above-mentioned causes.'

At the same time the story crops up in other quarters, so that we cannot look upon Otto as the inventor of the myth. The celebrated Maimonides alludes to it in a passage quoted by Joshua Lorki, a Jewish physician to Benedict XIII. Maimonides lived from 1135 to 1204. The passage is as follows: – 'It is evident both from the letters of Rambam (Maimonides), whose memory be blessed, and from the narration of merchants who have visited the ends of the earth, that at this time the root of our faith is to be found in the lands of Babel and Teman, where long ago Jerusalem was an exile; not reckoning those who live in the land of Paras and Madai, of the exiles of Schomrom, the number of which people is as the sand: of these some are still under the yoke of Paras, who is called the Great-Chief Sultan by the Arabs; others live in a place under the yoke of a strange people . . . governed by a Christian chief, Preste-Cuan by name. With him they have made a compact, and he with them; and this is a matter concerning which there can be no manner of doubt.'

Benjamin of Tudela, another Jew, travelled in the East between the years 1159–1173, the last being the date of his death. He wrote an account of his travels, and gives in it some information with regard to a mythical Jew king, who reigned in the utmost splendour over a realm inhabited by Jews alone, situate somewhere in the midst of a desert of vast extent. About this period there appeared a document which produced intense excitement throughout Europe – a letter, yes! a letter from the mysterious personage himself to Manuel Comnenus, Emperor of Constantinople (1143–1180) The exact date of this extraordinary epistle cannot be fixed with any certainty, but it certainly appeared before 1241, the date of the conclusion of the chronicle of Albericus Trium Fontium. This Albericus relates that in the year 1165 'Presbyter Joannes, the Indian king, sent his wonderful letter to various Christian princes, and especially to Manuel of Constantinople, and Frederic the Roman Emperor.' Similar letters were sent to Alexander III, to Louis VII of France, and to the King of Portugal, which are alluded to in chronicles and romances, and which were indeed turned into rhyme and sung all over Europe by minstrels and trouvères. The letter is as follows:–

'John, Priest by the Almighty power of God and the Might of our Lord Jesus Christ, King of Kings, and Lord of Lords, to his friend Emanuel, Prince of Constantinople, greeting, wishing him health, prosperity, and the continuance of Divine favour.

'Our Majesty has been informed that you hold our Excellency in love, and that the report of our greatness has reached you. Moreover we have heard through our treasurer that you have been pleased to send to us some objects of art and interest, that our Exaltedness might be gratified thereby.

'Being human, I receive it in good part, and we have ordered our treasurer to send you some of our articles in return.

'Now we desire to be made certain that you hold the right faith, and in all things cleave to Jesus Christ, our Lord, for we have heard that your court regard you as a god, though we know that you are mortal, and subject to human infirmities. . . . Should you desire to learn the greatness and excellency of our Exaltedness and of the land subject to our sceptre, then hear and believe: – I, Presbyter Johannes, the Lord of Lords, surpass all under heaven in virtue, in riches, and in power; seventy-two kings pay us tribute . . . In the three Indies our Magnificence rules, and our land extends beyond India, where rests the body of the holy Apostle Thomas; it reaches towards the sunrise over the wastes, and it trends towards deserted Babylon near the tower of Babel. Seventy-two provinces, of which only a few are Christian, serve us. Each has its own king, but all are tributary to us.

'Our land is the home of elephants, dromedaries, camels, crocodiles, meta-collinarum, cametennus, tensevetes, wild asses, white and red lions, white bears, white merles, crickets, griffins, tigers, lamias, hyænas, wild horses, wild oxen and wild men, men with horns, one-eyed, men with eyes before and behind, centaurs, fauns, satyrs, pygmies, forty-ell high giants, Cyclopses, and similar women; it is the home, too, of the phœnix, and of nearly all living animals. We have some people subject to us who feed on the flesh of men and of prematurely born animals, and who never fear death. When any of these people die, their friends and relations eat him ravenously, for they regard it as a main duty to munch human flesh. Their names are Gog and Magog, Anie, Agit, Azenach, Fommeperi, Befari, Conei-Samante, Agrimandri, Vintefolei, Casbei, Alanei. These and similar nations were shut in behind lofty mountains by Alexander the Great, towards the North. We lead them at our pleasure against our foes, and neither man nor beast is left undevoured, if our Majesty gives the requisite permission. And when all our foes are eaten, then we return with our hosts home again. These accursed fifteen nations will burst forth from the four quarters of the earth at the end of the world, in the times of Antichrist, and overrun all the abodes of the Saints as well as the great city Rome, which, by the way, we are prepared to give to our son who will be born, along with all Italy, Germany, the two Gauls, Britain and Scotland. We shall also give him Spain and all the land as far as the icy sea. The nations to which I have alluded, according to the words of the prophet, shall not stand in the judgment, on account of their offensive practices, but will be consumed to ashes by a fire which will fall on them from heaven.

'Our land streams with honey, and is overflowing with milk. In one region grows no poisonous herb, nor does a querulous frog ever quack in it, no scorpion exists, nor does the serpent glide amongst the grass, nor can any poisonous animals exist in it, or injure any one.

'Among the heathen, flows through a certain province the river Indus; encircling Paradise, it spreads its arms in manifold windings through the entire province. Here are found the emeralds, sapphires, carbuncles, topazes, chrysolites, onyxes, beryls, sardius, and other costly stones. Here grows the plant Assidos, which, when worn by any one, protects him from the evil spirit, forcing it to state its business and name; consequently the foul spirits keep out of the way there. In a certain land subject to us, all kinds of pepper is gathered, and is exchanged for corn and bread, leather and cloth. . . . At the foot of Mount Olympus bubbles up a spring which changes its flavour hour by hour, night and day, and the spring is scarcely three days' journey from Paradise, out of which Adam was driven. If any one has tasted thrice of the fountain from that day he will feel no fatigue, but will as long as he lives be as a man of thirty years. Here are found the small stones called Nudiosi, which, if borne about the body, prevent the sight from waxing feeble, and restore it where it is lost. The more the stone is looked at, the keener becomes the sight. In our territory is a certain waterless sea, consisting of tumbling billows of sand never at rest. None have crossed this sea; it lacks water altogether, yet fish are cast up upon the beach of various kinds, very tasty, and the like are nowhere else to be seen. Three days' journey from this sea are mountains from which rolls down a stony, waterless river, which opens into the sandy sea. As soon as the stream reaches the sea, its stones vanish in it and are never seen again. As long as the river is in motion, it cannot be crossed; only four days a week is it possible to traverse it. Between the sandy sea and the said mountains, in a certain plain is a fountain of singular virtue, which purges Christians and would-be Christians from all transgressions. The water stands four inches high in a hollow stone shaped like a mussel-shell. Two saintly old men watch by it, and ask the comers whether they are Christians, or are about to become Christians, then whether they desire healing with all their hearts. If they have answered well, they are bidden to lay aside their clothes, and to step into the mussel. If what they said be true, then the water begins to rise and gush over their heads;

thrice does the water thus lift itself, and every one who has entered the mussel leaves it cured of every complaint.

'Near the wilderness trickles between barren mountains a subterranean rill, which can only by chance be reached, for only occasionally the earth gapes, and he who would descend must do it with precipitation, ere the earth closes again. All that is gathered under the ground there is gem and precious stone. The brook pours into another river, and the inhabitants of the neighbourhood obtain thence abundance of precious stones. Yet they never venture to sell them without having first offered them to us for our private use: should we decline them, they are at liberty to dispose of them to strangers. Boys there are trained to remain three or four days under water, diving after the stones.

'Beyond the stone river are the ten tribes of the Jews, which, though subject to their own kings, are, for all that, our slaves and tributary to our Majesty. In one of our lands, hight Zone, are worms called in our tongue Salamanders. These worms can only live in fire, and they build cocoons like silkworms, which are unwound by the ladies of our palace, and spun into cloth and dresses, which are worn by our Exaltedness. These dresses in order to be cleaned and washed are cast into flames. . . . When we go to war, we have fourteen golden and bejewelled crosses borne before us instead of banners; each of these crosses is followed by 10,000 horsemen, and 100,000 foot soldiers fully armed, without reckoning those in charge of the luggage and provision.

'When we ride abroad plainly, we have a wooden, unadorned cross, without gold or gem about it, borne before us, in order that we may meditate on the sufferings of Our Lord Jesus Christ; also a golden bowl filled with earth, to remind us of that whence we sprung, and that to which we must return; but besides these there is borne a silver bowl full of gold, as a token to all that we are the Lord of Lords.

'All riches, such as are upon the world, our Magnificence possesses in super-abundance. With us no one lies, for he who speaks a lie is thenceforth regarded as dead; he is no more thought of, or honoured by us. No vice is tolerated by us. Every year we undertake a pilgrimage, with retinue of war, to the body of the holy prophet Daniel, which is near the desolated site of Babylon. In our realm fishes are caught, the blood of which dyes purple. The Amazons and the Brahmins are subject to us. The palace in which our Supereminency resides, is built after the pattern of the castle built by the Apostle Thomas for the Indian king Gundoforus. Ceilings, joists, and architrave are of Sethym wood, the roof of ebony, which can never catch fire. Over the gable of the palace are, at the extremities, two golden apples, in each of which are two carbuncles, so that the gold may shine by day, and the carbuncles by night. The greater gates of the palace are of sardius, with the horn of the horned snake inwrought, so that no one can bring poison within.

'The other portals are of ebony. The windows are of crystal; the tables are partly of gold, partly of amethyst, and the columns supporting the tables are partly of ivory, partly of amethyst. The court in which we watch the jousting is floored with onyx in order to increase the courage of the combatants. In the palace, at night, nothing is burned for light but wicks supplied with balsam. . . . Before our palace stands a mirror, the ascent to which consists of five and twenty steps of porphyry, and serpentine.' After a description of the gems adorning this mirror, which is guarded night and day by three thousand armed men, he explains its use: 'We look therein and behold all that is taking place in every province and region subject to our sceptre.

'Seven kings wait upon us monthly, in turn, with sixty-two dukes, two hundred and fifty-six counts and marquises: and twelve archbishops sit at table with us on our right, and twenty bishops on the left, besides the patriarch of S. Thomas, the Sarmatian Protopope, and the Archpope of Susa. . . . Our lord high steward is a primate and king, our cup-bearer is an archbishop and king, our chamberlain a bishop and king, our marshal a king and abbot.'

I may be spared further extracts from this extraordinary letter, which proceeds to describe the church in which Prester John worships, by enumerating the precious stones of which it is constructed, and their special virtues.

Whether this letter was in circulation before Pope Alexander wrote his, it is not easy to decide. Alexander does not allude to it, but speaks of the reports which have reached him of the piety and the magnificence of the Priest-King. At the same time, there runs a tone of bitterness through the letter, as though the Pope had been galled at the pretensions of this mysterious personage, and perhaps winced under the prospect of the man-eaters overrunning Italy, as suggested by John the Priest. The papal epistle is an assertion of the claims of the See of Rome to universal dominion, and it assures the Eastern Prince-Pope that his Christian professions are worthless, unless he submits to the successor of Peter. 'Not every one that saith unto me, Lord, Lord,' &c., quotes the Pope, and then explains that the will of God is that every monarch and prelate should eat humble pie to the Sovereign Pontiff.

Sir John Maundevil gives the origin of the priestly title of the Eastern despot, in his curious book of travels.

'So it befelle, that this emperour cam, with a Cristene knyght with him, into a chirche in Egypt: and it was Saterday in Wyttson woke. And the bishop made orders. And he beheld and listened the servyse fulle tenetyfly: and he asked the Cristene knyght, what men of degree thei scholden ben, that the prelate had before him. And the knyght answerede and seyde, that thei scholde ben prestes. And then the emperour seyde, that he wolde no longer ben clept kyng ne emperour, but preest: and that he wolde have the name of the first preest, that wente out of the chirche; and his name was John. And so evere more sittiens, he is clept Prestre John.'

It is probable that the foundation of the whole Prester-John myth lay in the report which reached Europe of the wonderful successes of Nestorianism in the East, and there seems reason to believe that the famous letter given above was a Nestorian fabrication. It certainly looks un-European; the gorgeous imagery is thoroughly Eastern, and the disparaging tone in which Rome is spoken of could hardly have been the expression of Western feelings. The letter has the object in view of exalting the East in religion and arts to an undue eminence at the expense of the West, and it manifests some ignorance of European geography, when it speaks of the land extending from Spain to the Polar Sea. Moreover, the sites of the patriarchates, and the dignity conferred on that of S. Thomas are indications of a Nestorian bias.

A brief glance at the history of this heretical Church may be of value here, as showing that there really was a foundation for the wild legends concerning a Christian empire in the East, so prevalent in Europe. Nestorius, a priest of Antioch and a disciple of S. Chrysostom, was elevated by the emperor to the patriarchate of Constantinople, and in the year 428 began to propagate his heresy, denying the hypostatic union. The Council of Ephesus denounced him, and, in spite of the emperor and court, Nestorius was anathematized and driven into exile. His sect spread through the East, and became a flourishing Church. It reached to China, where the emperor was all but converted; its missionaries traversed the frozen tundras of Siberia, preaching their maimed Gospel to the wild hordes which haunted those dreary wastes; it faced Buddhism and wrestled with it for the religious supremacy in Thibet; it established churches in Persia and in Bokhara; it penetrated India; it formed colonies in Ceylon, in Siam, and in Sumatra; so that the Catholicos or Pope of Bagdad exercised sway more extensive than that ever obtained by the successor of S. Peter. The number of Christians belonging to that communion probably exceeded that of the members of the true Catholic Church in East and West. But the Nestorian Church was not founded on the Rock, it rested on Nestorius, and when the rain descended, and the winds blew, and the floods came, and beat upon that house, it fell, leaving scarce a fragment behind.

Rubruquis the Franciscan, who in 1253 was sent on a mission into Tartary, was the first to let in a little light on the fable. He writes, 'The Catai dwelt beyond certain mountains across which I wandered, and in a plain in the midst of the mountains lived once an important Nestorian shepherd, who ruled over the Nestorian people, called Nayman. When Coir-Khan died, the Nestorian people raised this man to be king, and called him King Johannes, and related of him ten times as much as the truth. The Nestorians thereabouts have this way with them, that about nothing they make a great fuss, and thus they have got it noised abroad that Sartach, Mangu-Khan, and Ken-Khan were Christians, simply because they treated Christians well, and showed them more honour than other people. Yet, in fact, they were not Christians at all. And in like manner the story got about that there was a great King John. However, I traversed his pastures, and no one knew any thing about him, except a few Nestorians. In his pastures lives Ken-Khan, at whose court was Brother Andrew, whom I met on my way back. This Johannes had a brother, a famous shepherd, named Unc, who lived three weeks' journey beyond the mountains of Caracatais.'

This Unk-Khan was a real individual; he lost his life in the year 1203. Kuschhik, prince of the Nayman, and follower of Kor-Khan, fell in 1218.

Marco Polo, the Venetian traveller (1254–1324), identifies Unk-Khan with Prester John; he says, 'I will now tell you of the deeds of the Tartars, how they gained the mastery, and spread over the whole earth. The tartars dwelt between Georgia and Bargu, where there is a vast plain and level country, on which are neither cities nor forts, but capital pasturage and water. They had no chief of their own, but paid to Prester Johannes tribute. Of the greatness of this Prester Johannes, who was properly called Un-Khan, the whole world spake; the Tartars gave him one of every ten head of cattle. When Prester John noticed that they were increasing, he feared them, and planned how he could injure them. He determined therefore to scatter them, and he sent barons to do this. But the Tartars guessed what Prester John purposed . . . and they went away into the wide wastes of the North, where they might be beyond his reach.' He then goes on to relate how Tschengis-(Jenghiz-)Khan became the head of the Tartars, and how he fought against Prester John, and, after a desperate fight, overcame and slew him.

The Syriac Chronicle of the Jacobite Primate, Gregory Bar-Hebræus (born 1226, died 1286), also identifies Unk-Khan with Prester John. 'In the year of the Greeks 1514, of the Arabs 599 (A.D. 1202), when Unk-Khan, who is the Christian King John, ruled over a stock of the barbarian Hunns, called Kergis, Tschengys-Khan served him with great zeal. When John observed the superiority and serviceableness of the other, he envied him, and plotted to seize and murder him. But two sons of Unk-Khan, having heard this, told it to Tschengys, whereupon he and his comrades fled by night and secreted themselves. Next morning Unk-Khan took possession of the Tartar tents, but found them empty. Then the party of Tschengys fell upon him, and they met by the spring called Balschunah, and the side of Tschengys won the day; and the followers of Unk-Khan were compelled to yield. They met again several times, till Unk-Khan was utterly discomfited and was slain himself, and his wives, sons, and daughters carried into captivity. Yet we must consider that John, king of the Kergis, was not cast down for nought, nay rather because he had turned his heart from the fear of Christ his Lord, who had exalted him, and had taken a wife of the Zinish nation, called Quarakhata. Because he forsook the religion of his ancestors and followed strange gods, therefore God took the government from him, and gave it to one better than he, and whose heart was right before God.'

Some of the early travellers, such as John de Plano-Carpini and Marco Polo, in disabusing the popular mind of the belief in Prester John as a mighty Asiatic Christian monarch, unintentionally turned the popular faith in that individual into a new direction. They spoke of the black people of Abascia in Ethiopia, which, by the way, they called Middle India, as a great people subject to a Christian monarch.

Marco Polo says that the true monarch of Abyssinia is Christ; but that it is governed by six kings, three of whom are Christians and three Saracens, and that they are in league with the Soudan of Aden.

Bishop Jordanus, in his description of the world, accordingly sets down Abyssinia as the kingdom of Prester John; and such was the popular impression, which was confirmed by the appearance at intervals of ambassadors at European courts from the King of Abyssinia. The discovery of the Cape of Good Hope was due partly to a desire manifested in Portugal to open communications with this monarch, and King John II sent two men learned in Oriental languages through Egypt to the court of Abyssinia. The might and dominion of this prince, who had replaced the Tartar chief in the popular creed as Prester John, was of course greatly exaggerated, and was supposed to extend across Arabia and Asia to the wall of China. The spread of geographical knowledge has contracted the area of his dominions, and a critical acquaintance with history has exploded the myth which invested Unk-Khan the nomad chief with all the attributes of a demigod, uniting in one the utmost pretensions of a Pope and the proudest claims of a monarch.

CHAPTER 2

The Seven Sleepers of Ephesus

HE THEME of the Seven Sleepers – and of heroes or other famous people sleeping beneath hills and in caves – is one of the most popular myths of the Middle Ages. Gould mentions many examples, though he is curiously silent on the matter of King Arthur, of whom one of the most enduring stories of enchanted sleep is told. Indeed, the story appears to be connected with a number of sites in Britain, Wales and Scotland – notably Alderley Edge in Cheshire, Sewingshields Crags in Northumberland and the Eildon Hills on the Scottish borders – which Arthur shares with Thomas of Ercildoune (see below). The theme is part of an age-old and well-attested association of certain heroic people with the land on which they walked. This is best evidenced in Celtic tradition where the association of kings (especially of Ireland) with the land is such that they were said to mate with the spirit of the place in the form of a divine woman. In Arthur's case this has led to his being considered himself as the numen of the land of Britain, where he lies awaiting the call of his country to bring him back to fight again – the same story is recounted of Frederic Barbarossa in Germany and of William Tell in Switzerland.

In Wales the story is told about Arthur in very similar terms to that related by Gould of Barbarossa – a boy wanders into a cave and finds Arthur and seven of his knights asleep. The king's hair and fingernails have grown long, and a sword and a horn lie on a stone table at which he sits. The boy tries to draw the sword, at which the king raises his head and asks: 'Is it time?' In terror the youth runs away, leaving the king to resume his rest.

This story is not one that dates only from ancient times. It is still remarkably current. As recently as the early 1900s, when the famous General Kitchener was lost at sea, rumours persisted that he was not dead but had retreated into hiding, soon to emerge and lead the British armies to victory in the First World War. More recently still, when

18

the great statesman Sir Winston Churchill died, an old man watching the passing of the funeral processions was heard to remark that Churchill was not really dead but in hiding, and that he would return when his country needed him.

It seems that all of these stories spring in part from a desire to believe in the timely return of a great hero. In the case of King Arthur this had so strong a hold over the consciousness of the English people that Plantagenet King Edward I made a point of visiting the newly discovered 'grave' of Arthur at Glastonbury, and having the bones interred in a huge marble tomb – a clear statement that 'Arthur is dead. I am king.'

Curiously enough, in Celtic tradition Arthur is guilty of the same kind of act. An older myth is told of the semi-divine figure Bran the Blessed, who on his death had ordered his followers to bury his head beneath the White Mount in London with the face towards France. So long as it was there, he said, no invader would ever succeed in taking control of Britain. Arthur, in a fit of hubris, declared that only he would protect the land, and ordered the head dug up. Britain fell to a number of successive waves of conquest thereafter.

The Seven Sleepers themselves are, as Gould shows, well attested in a number of traditions. In parts of Arabia to this day pieces of paper with the names of the Sleepers – and their dog Katmir – are used to invoke protection upon a house. In the Norse legend the Sleepers are the sons of Mimer, who sleep in the Underworld guarding a treasure. Anyone who attempts to wake them perishes. They await the blowing of the horn that will signal the coming of Ragnarok, the last battle of the gods.

The number seven is itself highly significant. Apart from the Sleepers there are seven earths in Jewish Kabalah, the Seven Rishis of Hindu tradition, the seven sacred trees of Ireland, the Seven Pillars of Wisdom, and the Seven Champions of Christendom (all of them saints and therefore perhaps nearest to the Seven Sleepers). They are: St Andrew of Scotland, St Anthony of Italy, St David of Wales, St Denis of France, St George of England, St James of Spain and St Patrick of Ireland. Another list, namely of the Nine Christian Worthies, includes Arthur, Charlemagne, Alexander and Hector of Troy.

Ephesus was not the only site associated with the Sleepers. In Algeria they are said to have slept at N'gaous, while a cave in the Hirak Valley in Afghanistan was long known as the Valley of the Seven Sleepers.

* * *

ONE of the most picturesque myths of ancient days, is that which forms the subject of this article. It is thus told by Jacques de Voragine in his 'Legenda Aurea': –

'The seven sleepers were natives of Ephesus. The Emperor Decius, who persecuted the Christians, having come to Ephesus, ordered the erection of temples in the city, that all might come and sacrifice before him, and he commanded that the Christians should be sought out and given their choice, either to worship the idols, or to die. So great was the consternation in the city, that the friend denounced his friend, the father his son, and the son his father.

19

'Now there were in Ephesus seven Christians, Maximian, Malchus, Marcian, Dionysius, John, Serapion, and Constantine by name. These refused to sacrifice to the idols, and remained in their houses praying and fasting. They were accused before Decius, and they confessed themselves to be Christians. However, the emperor gave them a little time to consider what line they would adopt. They took advantage of this reprieve to dispense their goods among the poor, and then they retired, all seven, to Mount Celion, where they determined to conceal themselves.

'One of their number, Malchus, in the disguise of a physician, went to the town to obtain victuals. Decius, who had been absent from Ephesus for a little while, returned, and gave orders for the seven to be sought. Malchus, having escaped from the town, fled, full of fear, to his comrades, and told them of the emperor's fury. They were much alarmed; and Malchus handed them the loaves he had bought, bidding them eat, that, fortified by the food, they might have courage in the time of trial. They ate, and then, as they sat weeping and speaking to one another, by the will of God they fell asleep.

'The Pagans sought every where, but could not find them, and Decius was greatly irritated at their escape. He had their parents brought before him, and threatened them with death if they did not reveal the place of concealment; but they could only answer that the seven young men had distributed their goods to the poor, and that they were quite ignorant as to their whereabouts.

'Decius, thinking it possible that they might be hiding in a cavern, blocked up the mouth with stones, that they might perish of hunger.

'Three hundred and sixty years passed, and in the thirtieth year of the reign of Theodosius, there broke forth a heresy denying the resurrection of the dead. . . .

'Now, it happened that an Ephesian was building a stable on the side of Mount Celion, and finding a pile of stones handy, he took them for his edifice, and thus opened the mouth of the cave. Then the seven sleepers awoke, and it was to them as if they had slept but a single night. They began to ask Malchus what decision Decius had given concerning them.

'"He is going to hunt us down, so as to force us to sacrifice to the idols," was his reply. "God knows," replied Maximian, "we shall never do that." Then exhorting his companions, he urged Malchus to go back to the town to buy some more bread, and at the same time to obtain fresh information. Malchus took five coins and left the cavern. On seeing the stones, he was filled with astonishment; however, he went on towards the city; but what was his bewilderment, on approaching the gate, to see over it a cross! He went to another gate, and there he beheld the same sacred sign; and so he observed it over each gate of the city. He believed that he was suffering from the effects of a dream. Then he entered Ephesus, rubbing his eyes, and he walked to a baker's shop. He heard people using our Lord's name, and he was the more perplexed. "Yesterday, no one dared pronounce the name of Jesus, and now it is on every one's lips. Wonderful! I can hardly believe myself to be in Ephesus." He asked a passer-by the name of the city, and on being told it was Ephesus, he was thunderstruck. Now he entered a baker's shop, and laid down his money. The baker, examining the coin, inquired whether he had found a treasure, and began to whisper to some others in the shop. The youth, thinking that he was discovered, and that they were about to conduct him to the emperor, implored them to let him alone, offering to leave loaves and money if he might only be suffered to escape. But the shopmen, seizing him, said: "Whoever you are, you have found a treasure; show us where it is, that we may share it with you, and then we will hide you." Malchus was too frightened to answer. So they put a rope round his neck, and drew him through the streets into the market-place. The news soon spread that the young man had discovered a great treasure, and there was presently a vast crowd about him. He stoutly protested his innocence. No one recognized him, and his eyes ranging over the faces which surrounded him, could not see one which he had known, or which was in the slightest degree familiar to him.

'S. Martin, the bishop, and Antipater, the governor, having heard of the excitement, ordered the young man to be brought before them, along with the bakers.

"The bishop and the governor asked him where he had found the treasure, and he replied that he had found none, but that the few coins were from his own purse. He was next asked whence he came. He replied that he was a native of Ephesus, "if this be Ephesus".

'"Send for your relations – your parents, if they live here," ordered the governor.

'"They live here certainly," replied the youth; and he mentioned their names. No such names were known in the town. Then the governor exclaimed: "How dare you say that this money belonged to your parents when it dates back three hundred and seventy-seven years, and is as old as the beginning of the reign of Decius, and it is utterly unlike our modern coinage? Do you think to impose on the old men and sages of Ephesus? Believe me, I shall make you suffer the severities of the law unless you show where you made the discovery."

'"I implore you," cried Malchus, "in the name of God, answer me a few questions, and then I will answer yours! Where is the Emperor Decius gone to?"

'The bishop answered, "My son, there is no Emperor of that name; he who was thus called died long ago."

'Malchus replied, "All I hear perplexes me more and more. Follow me, and I will show you my comrades who fled with me into a cave of Mount Celion, only yesterday, to escape the cruelty of Decius. I will lead you to them."

'The bishop turned to the governor. "The hand of God is here," he said. Then they followed, and a great crowd after them. And Malchus entered first into the cavern to his companions, and the bishop after him. . . . And there they saw the martyrs seated in the cave, with their faces fresh and blooming as roses; so all fell down and glorified God. The bishop and the governor sent notice to Theodosius, and he hurried to Ephesus. All the inhabitants met him and conducted him to the cavern. As soon as the saints beheld the emperor, their faces shone like the sun, and the emperor gave thanks unto God, and embraced them, and said, "I see you, as though I saw the Saviour restoring Lazarus." Maximian replied, "Believe us! for the faith's sake, God has resuscitated us before the great resurrection day, in order that you may believe firmly in the resurrection of the dead. For as the child is in its mother's womb living and not suffering, so have we lived without suffering, fast asleep." And having thus spoken, they bowed their heads, and their souls returned to their Maker. The emperor, rising, bent over them and embraced them weeping. He gave orders for golden reliquaries to be made, but that night they appeared to him in a dream, and said that hitherto they had slept in the earth, and that in the earth they desired to sleep on till God should raise them again.'

Such is the beautiful story. It seems to have travelled to us from the East. Jacobus Sarugiensis a Mesopotamian bishop, in the fifth or sixth century, is said to have been the first to commit it to writing. Gregory of Tours was perhaps the first to introduce it to Europe. Dionysius of Antioch (ninth century) told the story in Syrian, and Photius of Constantinople reproduced it, with the remark that Mahomet had adopted it into the Koran. Metaphrastus alludes to it as well; in the tenth century Eutychius inserted it in his annals of Arabia; it is found in the Coptic and the Maronite books, and several early historians, as Paulus Diaconus, Nicephorus, &c., have inserted it in their works.

William of Malmesbury tells us a strange story concerning these sleepers. He says, that King Edward the Confessor sat, during the Easter festival, wearing his royal crown at dinner, in his palace of Westminster, surrounded by his bishops and nobles. During the banquet the king, instead of indulging in meat and drink, mused upon divine things, and sat long immersed in thought. Suddenly, to the astonishment of all present, he burst out laughing. After dinner, when he retired to his bedchamber to divest himself of his robes, three of his nobles, Earl Harold, who was afterwards king, and an abbot and a bishop, followed him, and asked the reason of his rare mirth. 'I saw,' said the pious monarch, 'things most wonderful to behold, and there-fore did I not laugh without a reason.' They entreated him to explain; and after musing for a while, he informed them that the Seven Sleepers of Ephesus, who had been slumbering two hundred years in a cavern of Mount Celion, lying always on their right sides, had of a sudden, turned themselves over on their left sides; that by heavenly favour he had seen them thus turn themselves, and at the sight he had been constrained to laugh. And as Harold and the abbot and bishop marvelled at his words, the king related to them the story of the Seven Sleepers, with the shape and proportion of their several bodies, which wonderful things no man had as yet committed to writing; nay, he spake of the Ephesian sleepers, as though he had always dwelt with them. Earl Harold, on hearing this, got ready a knight, a clerk and a monk, who were forthwith sent to the emperor at Constantinople, with letters and presents from King Edward. By the emperor these messengers were forwarded to Ephesus with letters to the Bishop, commanding him to admit the three English-men into the cavern of the sleepers. And, lo! it fell out even as the king had seen in vision. For the Ephesians declared that they knew from their forefathers that the Seven had ever lain on their right sides; but on the entry of the Englishmen into the cave, they were all found lying on their left sides. And this was a warning of the miseries which were to befall Christendom through the inroads of the Saracens, Turks and Tartars. For whenever sorrow threatens, the Sleepers turn on their sides.

A poem on the Seven Sleepers was composed by a trouvère named Chardri, and is mentioned by M. Fr. Michel in his 'Rapports au Ministre de l'Instruction Public'; a German poem on the same subject, of the thirteenth century, in 935 verses, has been published by M. Karajan; and the Spanish poet, Augustin Morreto, composed a drama on it, entitled 'Los Siete Durmientes', which is inserted in the 19th volume of the rare work 'Comedias Nuevas Escogidas de los Mejores Ingenios'; last, and not least, it has formed the subject of a poem by the late Dr Neale.

Mahomet has somewhat improved on the story. He has made the Sleepers prophesy his coming, and he has given them a dog named Kratim, or Kratimer, which sleeps with them, and which is endowed with the gift of prophecy.

As a special favour this dog is to be one of the ten animals to be admitted into his paradise, the others being Jonah's whale, Solomon's ant, Ishmael's ram, Abraham's calf, the Queen of Sheba's ass, the prophet Salech's camel, Moses' ox, Belkis' cuckoo, and Mahomet's ass.

It was perhaps too much for the Seven Sleepers to ask, that their bodies should be left to rest in earth. In ages when saintly relics were valued above gold and precious stones, their request was sure to be shelved; and so we find that their remains were conveyed to Marseilles in a large stone sarcophagus, which is still exhibited in S. Victor's Church. In the Musæum Victorium at Rome is a curious and ancient representation of them in a cement of sulphur and plaster. Their names are engraved beside them, together with certain attributes. Near Constantine and John are two clubs, near Maximian a knotty club, near Malchus and Martinian two axes, near Serapion a burning torch, and near Danesius or Dionysius a great nail, such as those spoken of by Horace and S. Paulinus as having been used for torture.

In this group of figures, the seven are represented as young, without beards, and indeed in ancient martyrologies they are frequently called boys.

It has been inferred from this curious plaster representation, that the seven may have suffered under Decius, A.D. 250, and have been buried in the aforementioned cave; whilst the discovery and translation of their relics under Theodosius, in 479, may have given rise to the fable. And this I think probable enough. The story of long sleepers and the number seven connected with it is ancient enough, and dates from heathen mythology.

Like many another ancient myth, it was laid hold of by Christian hands and baptized.

Pliny relates the story of Epimenides the epic poet, who, when tending his sheep one hot day, wearied and oppressed with slumber, retreated into a cave, where he fell asleep. After fifty-seven years he awoke, and found every thing changed. His brother, whom he had left a stripling, was now a hoary man.

Epimenides was reckoned one of the seven sages by those who exclude Periander. He flourished in the time of Solon. After his death, at the age of two hundred and eighty-nine, he was revered as a God, and honoured especially by the Athenians.

This story is a version of the older legend of the perpetual sleep of the shepherd Endymion, who was thus preserved in unfading youth and beauty by Jupiter.

According to an Arabic legend, S. George thrice rose from his grave, and was thrice slain.

In Scandinavian mythology we have Siegfrid or Sigurd thus resting, and awaiting his call to come forth and fight. Charlemagne sleeps in the Odenberg in Hess, or in the Untersberg near Salzburg, seated on his throne, with his crown on his head and his sword at his side, waiting till the times of Antichrist are fulfilled, when he will wake and burst forth to avenge the blood of the saints. Ogier the Dane, or Olger Dansk, will in like manner shake off his slumber and come forth from the dream-land of Avallon to avenge the right – oh that he had shown himself in the Schleswig-Holstein war!

Well do I remember, as a child, contemplating with wondering awe the great Kyffhäuserberg in Thuringia, for therein, I was told, slept Frederic Barbarossa and his six knights. A shepherd once penetrated into the heart of the mountain by a cave, and discovered therein a hall where sat the Emperor at a stone table, and his red beard had grown through the slab. At the tread of the shepherd, Frederic awoke from his slumber, and asked, 'Do the ravens still fly over the mountains?'

'Sire! they do.'

'Then we must sleep another hundred years.'

But when his beard has wound itself thrice round the table, then will the Emperor awake with his knights, and rush forth to release Germany from its bondage, and exalt it to the first place among the kingdoms of Europe.

In Switzerland slumber three Tells at Rütli near the Vierwaldstätter-see, waiting for the hour of their country's direst need. A shepherd crept into the cave where they rest. The third Tell rose and asked the time. 'Noon,' replied the shepherd lad. 'The time is not yet come,' said Tell, and lay down again.

In Scotland, beneath the Eildon hills, sleeps Thomas of Erceldoune; the murdered French who fell in the Sicilian Vespers at Palermo, are also slumbering till the time is come when they may wake to avenge themselves. When Constantinople fell into the hands of the Turks, a priest was celebrating the sacred mysteries at the great silver altar of S. Sophia. The celebrant cried to God to protect the sacred host from profanation. Then the wall opened, and he entered, bearing the Blessed Sacrament. It closed on him, and there he is sleeping with his head bowed before the Body of Our Lord, waiting till the Turk is cast out of Constantinople, and S. Sophia is released from its profanation. God speed the time!

In Bohemia sleep three miners deep in the heart of the Kuttenberg. In North America, Ripp Van Winkle passed twenty years slumbering in the Katskill mountains. In Spain, Boabdil el Chico, the last Arab king of Granada, is said to lie spellbound in the mountains close to the Alhambra. In Arabia, the prophet Elijah waits till he is called forth in the days of Antichrist. In Ireland, Brian Boroimhe slumbers, waiting till a Fenian insurrection promising action and not talk summons him to his country's aid. In Wales, the legend of Arthur still dreaming through a long sleep in Avillon, has not died out. In Servia, Knez Lazar, who fell in battle against the Turks in the fight of Kossowa, in 1389, is expected to re-appear one day. A similar hope of the return of James IV lasted for more than a hundred years after Flodden was fought. In Portugal it is believed that Sebastian, the chivalrous young monarch who did his best to ruin his country by his rash invasion of Morocco, is sleeping somewhere, but he will wake again to be his country's deliverer in the hour of need. Olaf Tryggvason is waiting a similar occasion in Norway. Even Napoleon Bonaparte is believed among some of the French peasantry to be sleeping on in a like manner.

S. Hippolytus relates that S. John the Divine is slumbering at Ephesus, and Sir John Mandeville relates the circumstances as follows: 'From Pathmos men gone unto Ephesim, a fair citee and nyghe to the see. And there dyede Seynte Johne, and was buryed behynde the highe Awtiere, in a toumbe. And there is a faire chirche. For Christene mene weren wont to holden that place alweyes. And in the tombe of Seynt John is noughte but manna, that is clept Aungeles mete. For his body was translated into Paradys. And Turkes holden now alle that place and the citee and the Chirche. And all Asie the lesse is yclept Turkye. And ye shalle undrestond, that Seynt Johne bid make his grave there in his Lyf, and leyd himself there-inne all quyk. And therefore somme men seyn, that he dyed noughte, but that he resteth there till the Day of Doom. And forsoothe there is a gret marveule: For men may see there the erthe of the tombe apertly many tymes steren and moven, as there weren quykke thinges undre.' The connexion of this legend of S. John with Ephesus may have had something to do with turning the seven martyrs of that city into seven sleepers.

The annals of Iceland relate that in 1403, a Finn of the name of Fethmingr, living in Halogaland, in the North of Norway, happening to enter a cave, fell asleep, and woke not for three whole years, lying with his bow and arrows at his side, untouched by bird or beast.

There certainly are authentic accounts of persons having slept for an extraordinary length of time, but I shall not mention any, as I believe the legend we are considering, not to have been an exaggeration of facts, but a Christianized myth of paganism. The fact of the number seven being so prominent in many of the tales, seems to lead to this conclusion. Barbarossa changes his position every seven years. Charlemagne starts in his chair at similar intervals. Olger Dansk stamps his iron mace on the floor once every seven years. Olaf Redbeard in Sweden uncloses his eyes at precisely the same distances of time.

I believe that the mythological core of this picturesque legend is the repose of the earth through the seven winter months. In the North Frederic and Charlemagne certainly replace Odin.

The German and Scandinavian still heathen legends represent the heroes as about to issue forth for the defence of Fatherland in the hour of direst need. The converted and Christianized tale brings the martyr youths forth in the hour when a heresy is afflicting the Church, that they may destroy the heresy by their witness to the truth of the Resurrection.

If there is something majestic in the heathen myth, there is singular grace and beauty in the Christian tale, teaching as it does such a glorious doctrine; but it is surpassed in delicacy by the modern form which the same myth has assumed – a form which is a real transformation, leaving the doctrine taught the same. It has been made into a romance by Hoffman, and is versified by Trinius. I may perhaps be allowed to translate with some freedom the poem of the latter: –

> In an ancient shaft of Falum,
>   Year by year a body lay,
> God-preserved, as though a treasure,
>   Kept unto the waking day.
>
> Not the turmoil, nor the passions,
>   Of the busy world o'erhead,
> Sounds of war, or peace rejoicings,
>   Could disturb the placid dead.
>
> Once a youthful miner, whistling,
>   Hew'd the chamber, now his tomb,
> Crash! the rocky fragments tumbled,
>   Closed him in abysmal gloom.
>
> Sixty years pass'd by, ere miners
>   Toiling, hundred fathoms deep,
> Broke upon the shaft where rested
>   That poor miner in his sleep.
>
> As the gold-grains lie untarnish'd
>   In the dingy soil and sand,
> Till they gleam and flicker, stainless,
>   In the digger's sifting hand;
>
> As the gem in virgin brilliance
>   Rests, till usher'd into day; –

26

So uninjured, uncorrupted,
    Fresh and fair the body lay.

And the miners bore it upward,
    Laid it in the yellow sun,
Up, from out the neighb'ring houses,
    Fast the curious peasants run.

'Who is he?' with eyes they question.
    'Who is he?' they ask aloud:
Hush! a wizen'd old hag comes hobbling,
    Panting through the wondr'ing crowd.

Oh! the cry – half joy, half sorrow –
    As she flings her at his side,
'John! the sweetheart of my girlhood,
    Here am I, am I, thy bride.

'Time on thee has left no traces,
    Death from wear has shielded thee;
I am aged, worn, and wasted,
    Oh! what life has done to me!

Then, his smooth unfurrow'd forehead
    Kiss'd that ancient wither'd crone;
And the Death which had divided,
    Now united them in one.

CHAPTER 3

The Dog Gellert

BARING-GOULD demonstrates very thoroughly the wide dissemination of this story, which appears in a number of versions throughout Europe and both the Middle and Far East. A version which he misses is to be found within the fascinating thirteenth-century Arthurian romance *Arthur and Gorlagon*. In this story a man is turned into a werewolf by his faithless wife and, in his subsequent wanderings, is befriended by a king whose constant companion he becomes. Then, one day, the king goes to visit a neighbouring monarch and leaves the wolf in the care of his queen. Unknown to the king, she is as faithless as the man-wolf's own wife and secretly arranges to meet her lover – one of the king's serving-men. When the wolf sees this it attacks the man and savages him. The queen, in desperation, invents a story of the wolf's having attacked her and the king's young son, and of the brave servant trying to protect them. She then takes the child to a hidden room and shuts him up there. When the king returns she tells him that the wolf has not only savaged the servant but also killed the child. The king is naturally overwhelmed with grief and anger, but the wolf greets him with such affection and gentleness that he is given pause. The man-wolf then drags him down to the hidden room and reveals that his son is still alive. The truth is revealed and the wolf vindicated.

Here the wolf is not slain as in the story of Gellert, but the underlying theme, of a faithful animal (in this case a man who has been given the shape of an animal) which is suspected of having killed its master's child but is subsequently proved to be innocent, is clearly present.

Another related theme is that of 'the calumniated wife' – a widespread motif in many parts of the world. It is best known in the West from its inclusion in the Celtic story of the hero Pryderi, whose mother Rhiannon is likewise falsely accused of having killed and eaten her children – the real culprit being a monster – and who is made to suffer

a terrible punishment for a crime of which she was innocent. Here the story is inverted, but again the underlying theme is of an accusation which is revealed in time to be false.

Gould's closing remarks concerning the wide dissemination of certain stories of this kind are interesting, as is the study of the themes which reoccur in folk literature and myth the world over. The folklorist Arne Stith-Thompson listed over ten thousand such motifs and classified them all in his monumental *Folk-Motif Index*. The story of 'the man who killed his dog' is among them and although it is remembered in the story of Gellert by the inhabitants of the little Welsh village of Beddgelert (Gelert's Grave) in Gwynedd, the truth is that less than two hundred years ago the 'grave' did not exist. It was constructed by a man named David Pritchard, who moved to the village in 1793 and adapted the tale to this new setting. Prompted perhaps by the old Welsh proverb 'As foolish as the man who slew his greyhound', Pritchard, with the help of the parish clerk, erected the 'grave' himself. The name Gellert seems to have been his own invention also, derived from the original name of the village, which was then called Bethcelert or Beddcilart after an early Celtic warrior named Celert. Prince Llewellyn was introduced into the story because of his association with a nearby Augustinian abbey.

Thus was this 'new' version of an old tale created. Pritchard also told the tale to the poet William Spencer, whose ballad version of the story made it known to an even wider audience. The site can still be visited today, though few who go there are aware of the true history of the place.

*   *   *

HAVING demolished the story of the famous shot of William Tell, I proceed to the destruction of another article of popular belief.

Who that has visited Snowdon has not seen the grave of Llewellyn's faithful hound Gellert, and been told by the guide the touching story of the death of the noble animal? How can we doubt the facts, seeing that the place, Beth-Gellert, is named after the dog, and that the grave is still visible? But unfortunately for the truth of the legend, its pedigree can be traced with the utmost precision.

The story is as follows: –

The Welsh Prince Llewellyn had a noble deerhound, Gellert, whom he trusted to watch the cradle of his baby son whilst he himself was absent.

One day, on his return, to his intense horror, he beheld the cradle empty and upset, the clothes dabbled with blood, and Gellert's mouth dripping with gore. Concluding hastily that the hound had proved unfaithful, had fallen on the child and devoured it, – in a paroxysm of rage the prince drew his sword and slew the dog. Next instant the cry of the babe from behind the cradle showed him that the child was uninjured, and, on looking further, Llewellyn discovered the body of a huge wolf, which had entered the house to seize and devour the child, but which had been kept off and killed by the brave dog Gellert.

In his self-reproach and grief, the prince erected a stately monument to Gellert, and called the place where he was buried after the poor hound's name.

Now, I find in Russia precisely the same story told, with just the same appearance of truth, of a Czar Piras. In Germany it appears with considerable variations. A man determines on slaying his old dog Sultan, and consults with his wife how this is to be effected. Sultan overhears the conversation, and complains bitterly to the wolf, who suggests an ingenious plan by which the master may be induced to spare his dog. Next day, when the man is going to his work, the wolf undertakes to carry off the child from its cradle. Sultan is to attack him and rescue the infant. The plan succeeds admirably, and the dog spends his remaining years in comfort.

But there is a story in closer conformity to that of Gellert among the French collections of fabliaux made by Le Grand d'Aussy and Edélestand du Méril. It became popular through the 'Gesta Romanorum', a collection of tales made by the monks for harmless reading, in the fourteenth century.

In the 'Gesta' the tale is told as follows: –

'Folliculus, a knight, was fond of hunting and tournaments. He had an only son, for whom three nurses were provided. Next to this child, he loved his falcon and his greyhound. It happened one day that he was called to a tournament, whither his wife and domestics went also, leaving the child in the cradle, the greyhound lying by him, and the falcon on his perch. A serpent that inhabited a hole near the castle, taking advantage of the profound silence that reigned, crept from his habitation, and advanced towards the cradle to devour the child. The falcon perceiving the danger, fluttered with his wings till he awoke the dog, who instantly attacked the invader, and after a fierce conflict, in which he was sorely wounded, killed him. He then lay down on the ground to lick and heal his wounds. When the nurses returned, they found the cradle overturned, the child thrown out, and the ground covered with blood, as was also the dog, who they immediately concluded had killed the child.

'Terrified at the idea of meeting the anger of the parents, they determined to escape; but in their flight fell in with their mistress, to whom they were compelled to relate the supposed murder of the child by the greyhound. The knight soon arrived to hear the sad story, and, maddened with fury, rushed forward to the spot. The poor wounded and faithful animal made an effort to rise and welcome his master with his accustomed fondness, but the enraged knight received him on the point of his sword, and he fell lifeless to the ground. On examination of the cradle, the infant was found alive, and unhurt, with the dead serpent lying by him. The knight now perceived what had happened, lamented bitterly over his faithful dog, and blamed himself for having too hastily depended on the words of his wife. Abandoning the profession of arms, he broke his lance in pieces, and vowed a pilgrimage to the Holy Land, where he spent the rest of his days in peace.'

The monkish hit at the wife is amusing, and might have been supposed to have originated with those determined misogynists, as the gallant Welshmen lay all the blame on the man. But the good compilers of the 'Gesta' wrote little of their own, except moral applications of the tales they relate, and the story of Folliculus and his dog, like many others in their collection, is drawn from a foreign source.

It occurs in the Seven Wise Masters, and in the 'Calumnia Novercalis' as well, so that it must have been popular throughout Mediæval Europe. Now the tales of the Seven Wise Masters are translations from a Hebrew work, the Kalilah and Dimnah of Rabbi Joel, composed about A.D. 1250, or from Symeon Seth's Greek Kylile and Dimne, written in 1080. These Greek and Hebrew works were derived from kindred sources. That of Rabbi Joel was a translation from an Arabic version made by

Nasr-Allah in the twelfth century, whilst Simeon Seth's was a translation of the Persian Kalilah and Dimnah. But the Persian Kalilah and Dimnah was not either an original work, it was in turn a translation from the Sanskrit Pantschatantra, made about A.D. 540.

In this ancient Indian book the story runs as follows –

A Brahmin named Devasaman had a wife, who gave birth to a son, and also to an ichneumon. She loved both her children dearly, giving them alike the breast, and anointing them alike with salves. But she feared the ichneumon might not love his brother.

One day, having laid her boy in bed, she took up the water jar, and said to her husband, 'Hear me, master! I am going to the tank to fetch water. Whilst I am absent watch the boy, lest he gets injured by the ichneumon.' After she had left the house, the Brahmin went forth begging, leaving the house empty. In crept a black snake, and attempted to bite the child; but the ichneumon rushed at it, and tore it in pieces. Then proud of its achievement, it sallied forth, all bloody, to meet its mother. She, seeing the creature stained with blood, concluded, with feminine precipitance, that it had fallen on the baby and killed it, and she flung her water jar at it and slew it. Only on her return home did she ascertain her mistake.

The same story is also told in the Hitopadesa, but the animal is an otter, not an ichneumon. In the Arabic version a weasel takes the place of the ichneumon.

The Buddhist missionaries carried the story into Mongolia, and in the Mongolian Uligerun, which is a translation of the Tibetian Dsanglun, the story reappears with the pole-cat as the brave and suffering defender of the child.

Stanislaus Julien, the great Chinese scholar, has discovered the same tale in the Chinese work entitled, 'The Forest of Pearls from the Garden of the Law'. This work dates from 668; and in it the creature is an ichneumon.

In the Persian Sindibad-nâmeh, is the same tale, but the faithful animal is a cat. In Sandabar and Syntipas it has become a dog. Through the influence of Sandabar on the Hebrew translation of the Kalilah and Dimnah, the ichneumon is also replaced by a dog.

Such is the history of the Gellert legend; it is an introduction into Europe from India, every step of its transmission being clearly demonstrable. From the Gesta Romanorum it passed into a popular tale throughout Europe, and in different countries it was, like the Tell myth, localized and individualized. Many a Welsh story, such as those contained in the Mabinogion, are as easily traced to an Eastern origin.

But every story has its root. The root of the Gellert tale is this: A man forms an alliance of friendship with a beast or bird. The dumb animal renders him a signal service. He misunderstands the act, and kills his preserver.

We have tracked this myth under the Gellert form from India to Wales; but under another form it is the property of the whole Aryan family, and forms a portion of the traditional lore of all nations sprung from that stock.

Thence arose the classic fable of the peasant, who, as he slept, was bitten by a fly. He awoke, and in a rage killed the insect. When too late he observed that the little creature had aroused him that he might avoid a snake which lay coiled up near his pillow.

In the Anvar-i-Suhaili is the following kindred tale. A king had a falcon. One day, whilst hunting, he filled a goblet with water dropping from a rock. As he put the vessel to his lips, his falcon dashed upon it, and upset it with its wings. The king, in a fury, slew the bird, and then discovered that the water dripped from the jaws of a serpent of the most poisonous description.

This story, with some variations, occurs in Æsop, Ælian, and Apthonius. In the Greek fable, a peasant liberates an eagle from the clutches of a dragon. The dragon spirts poison into the water which the peasant is about to drink, without observing what the monster had done. The grateful eagle upsets the goblet with his wings.

The story appears in Egypt under a whimsical form. A Wali once smashed a pot full of herbs which a cook had prepared. The exasperated cook thrashed the well-intentioned but unfortunate Wali within an inch of his life, and when he returned, exhausted with his efforts at belabouring the man, to examine the broken pot, he discovered amongst the herbs a poisonous snake.

How many brothers, sisters, uncles, aunts, and cousins of all degrees a little story has! And how few of the tales we listen to can lay any claim to originality? There is scarcely a story which I hear, which I cannot connect with some family of myths, and whose pedigree I cannot ascertain with more or less precision. Shakespeare drew the plots of his plays from Boccaccio or Straparola; but these Italians did not invent the tales they lent to the English dramatist. King Lear does not originate with Geoffry of Monmouth, but comes from early Indian stores of fable, whence also are derived the Merchant of Venice and the pound of flesh, aye! and the very incident of the three caskets.

But who would credit it, were it not proved by conclusive facts, that Johnny Sands is the inheritance of the whole Aryan family of nations, and that Peeping Tom of Coventry peeped in India and on the Tartar steppes ages before Lady Godiva was born?

If you listen to 'Traviata' at the opera, you have set before you a tale which has lasted for centuries, and which was perhaps born in India.

If you read in classic fable of Orpheus charming woods and meadows, beasts and birds, with his magic lyre, you remember to have seen the same fable related in the Kalewala of the Finnish Wainomainen, and in the Kaleopoeg of the Esthonian Kalewa.

If you take up English history and read of William the Conqueror slipping as he landed on British soil, and kissing the earth, saying he had come to greet and claim his own, you remember that the same story is told of Napoleon in Egypt, of King Olaf Harald's son in Norway, and in classic history of Junius Brutus on his return from the oracle.

A little while ago I cut out of a Sussex newspaper, a story purporting to be the relation of a fact which had taken place at a fixed date in Lewes. This was the story. A tyrannical husband locked the door against his wife, who was out having tea with a neighbour, gossiping and scandalmongering; when she applied for admittance, he pretended not to know her. She threatened to jump into the well unless he opened the door.

The man, not supposing that she would carry her threat into execution, declined, alleging that he was in bed, and the night was chilly; besides which he entirely disclaimed all acquaintance with the lady who besought admittance.

The wife then flung a log into a well, and secreted herself behind the door. The man hearing the splash, fancied that his good lady was really in the deeps, and forth he darted in his nocturnal costume, which was of the lightest, to ascertain whether his deliverance was complete. At once the lady darted into the house, locked the door, and on the husband pleading for admittance, she declared most solemnly from the window that she did not know *him*.

Now this story, I can positively assert, unless the events of this world move in a circle, did not happen in Lewes, or any other Sussex town.

It was told in the Gesta Romanorum six hundred years ago, and it was told, may be, as many hundred years before in India, for it is still to be found in Sanskrit collections of tales.

CHAPTER 4

Antichrist and Pope Joan

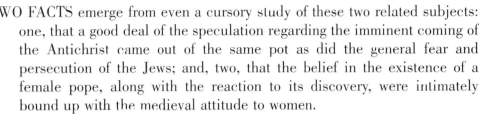

WO FACTS emerge from even a cursory study of these two related subjects: one, that a good deal of the speculation regarding the imminent coming of the Antichrist came out of the same pot as did the general fear and persecution of the Jews; and, two, that the belief in the existence of a female pope, along with the reaction to its discovery, were intimately bound up with the medieval attitude to women.

Literature on the theme of Antichrist is vast, and at various times contenders for the title have included just about everyone who has ever contradicted the Catholic Church. At one time the philosopher Mani (originator of the medieval 'heretical' sect of Manichaeans) was dubbed Antichrist, and was described as numbering among his followers a set of disciples who were the exact polar opposite of the twelve Apostles of Christ. From the thirteenth century onwards, most texts which included the story of Merlin depicted him as the product of a failed attempt to engender Antichrist on a human woman, with numerous salacious descriptions of the demonic seduction of Merlin's mother. When the child is born he is covered all over with coarse black hair – a legacy of his paternal parent – and is hastily baptized, at which point the body-hair falls from him. Merlin subsequently retained the magical power of his father, but put it to the service of good by helping King Arthur. The reality of the story probably originated in the notion of Merlin having been born from the union of a human woman and a faery being – the latter being perceived as evil by the medieval monks who composed the later versions of the story.

The notion of Antichrist is still with us, however, recurring in contemporary form in such films as the *Omen* series.

Baring-Gould is highly sceptical as to any possible authenticity of the subject of Joan; and, indeed, most of the commentators who have seen fit to write about the female pope have been similarly dismissive. On the face of it the dates alone would seem to suggest that a Pope John VIII (the supposed pseudonym taken by Joan) could not have ruled over the Vatican at the times stated, since the dates of the popes who ruled before and after are known. However, it would not be the first time that such dates had been altered to fit desired facts, and it seems to me that there is no reason to doubt that such a figure ever existed. Nor should one ignore the fact that the story attained such currency during the Middle Ages that, to this day, modern popes on the way to and from their installation turn aside at the place in the street where the infamous 'Papess' is supposed to have given birth to her child. Also, until at least as recently as the nineteenth century, the sex of papal candidates was checked before they were allowed to stand for the office. A Latin joke circulated among the people of Italy for many years: 'Non papa sed mama' (Not a pope [father] but a mother).

It has been suggested that the origin of the story was either a Roman folk-tale or a confusion over a statue which once stood in the Vatican. This probably represented a priest of Mithras carrying a child. The inscription, being unintelligible, was mistakenly read as the epitaph to a female pope. The strength of the idea may be guessed at from the fact that all traditional Tarot packs still include 'The Papess', suggesting that the origins of the figure may well date back to pre-Christian times, as does much of the symbolism of the Tarot. The earliest surviving packs suggest that the original figure may have been either one of the Greek Muses or a later, Renaissance, figure representing one of the seven Liberal Arts.

Despite every effort to dismiss the story as nonsense, controversy has continued to follow the idea of the female pope. In 1866 a novel on the subject was published in Athens by the Greek writer Emmanuel Royidis. It became an immediate best-seller and earned its author excommunication from the Catholic Church, while a papal ban was placed on the book itself. A sensitive and clever work, it can still be read with pleasure today in the wise and witty translation of one of the twentieth century's greatest authors, Lawrence Durrell.

*   *   *

FROM the earliest ages of the Church, the advent of the Man of Sin has been looked forward to with terror, and the passages of Scripture relating to him have been studied with solemn awe, lest that day of wrath should come upon the Church unawares. As events in the world's history took place which seemed to be indications of the approach of Antichrist, a great horror fell upon men's minds, and their imaginations conjured up myths which flew from mouth to mouth, and which were implicitly believed.

Before speaking of these strange tales which produced such an effect on the minds of men in the Middle Ages, it will be well briefly to examine the opinions of divines of the early ages on the passages of Scripture connected with the coming of the last great persecutor of the Church. Antichrist was believed by most ancient writers to be destined to arise out of the tribe of Dan, a belief founded on the prediction of Jacob, 'Dan shall be a serpent by the way, an adder in the path', and on the exclamation of the dying patriarch, when looking on his son Dan, 'I have waited for Thy Salvation, O Lord,' as though the long-suffering of God had borne long with that tribe, but in vain, and it was to be extinguished without hope. This, indeed, is implied in the sealing of the servants of God, in their foreheads, when twelve thousand out of every tribe, except Dan, were seen by S. John to receive the seal of adoption, whilst of the tribe of Dan *not one* was sealed, as though it, to a man, had apostatized.

Opinions as to the nature of Antichrist were divided. Some held that he was to be a devil in phantom body, and of this number was Hippolytus. Others again believed that he would be an incarnate demon, true man and true devil; in fearful and diabolical parody of the Incarnation of our Lord. A third view was that he would be merely a desperately wicked man, acting upon diabolic inspirations, just as the saints act upon divine inspirations. S. John Damascene expressly asserts that he will not be an incarnate demon, but a devilish man, for he says, 'Not as Christ assumed humanity, so will the devil become human, but the Man will receive all the inspiration of Satan, and will suffer the devil to take up his abode within him.' In this manner, Antichrist could have many forerunners, and so S. Jerome and S. Augustine saw an Antichrist in Nero, not *the* Antichrist, but one of those of whom the Apostle speaks – 'Even now are there many Antichrists.' Thus also every enemy of the faith, such as Diocletian, Julian, and Mahomet, has been regarded as a precursor of the Arch-persecutor, who was expected to sum up in himself the cruelty of a Nero or Diocletian, the show of virtue of a Julian, and the spiritual pride of a Mahomet.

From infancy the evil one is to take possession of Antichrist, and to train him for his office, instilling into him cunning, cruelty, and pride. His doctrine will be – not downright infidelity, but a 'show of godliness', whilst 'denying the power thereof', i.e. the miraculous origin and divine authority of Christianity. He will sow doubts of our Lord's manifestation 'in the flesh', he will allow Christ to be an excellent Man, capable of teaching the most exalted truths, and inculcating the purest morality, yet Himself fallible and carried away by fanaticism.

In the end, however, Antichrist will 'exalt himself to sit as God in the temple of God', and become 'the abomination of desolation standing in the holy place'. At the same time there is to be an awful alliance struck between himself, the impersonification of the world-power, and the Church of God; some high pontiff of which, or the episcopacy in general, will enter into league with the unbelieving State to oppress the very elect. It is a strange instance of religionary virulence which makes some detect the Pope of Rome in the Man of Sin, the Harlot, the Beast, and the Priest going before it. The Man of Sin and the Beast are unmistakably identical, and refer to an Antichristian world-power; whilst the Harlot and the Priest are symbols of an apostasy in the Church. There is nothing Roman in this, but something very much the opposite.

How the Abomination of Desolation can be considered as set up in a Church where every sanctuary is adorned with all that can draw the heart to the Crucified, and raise the thoughts to the imposing ritual of heaven, is a puzzle to me. To the man uninitiated in the law that Revelation is to be interpreted by contraries, it would seem more like the Abomination of Desolation in the Holy Place if he entered a Scotch Presbyterian, or a Dutch Calvinist, place of worship. Rome does not fight against the Daily Sacrifice, and endeavour to abolish it; that has been rather the labour of so-called Church Reformers, who with the suppression of the doctrine of Eucharistic Sacrifice and Sacramental Adoration have well nigh obliterated all notion of worship to be addressed to the God-Man. Rome does not deny the power of the godliness of which she makes show, but insists on that power with no broken accents. It is rather in other communities, where authority is flung aside, and any man is permitted to believe or reject what he likes, that we must look for the leaven of the Antichristian spirit at work. However, this is not a question into which we care to enter, our province is myth not theology.

In the time of Antichrist, we are told by ancient Commentators, the Church will be divided: one portion will hold to the world-power, the other will seek out the old paths, and cling to the only true Guide. The high places will be filled with unbelievers in the Incarnation, and the Church will be in a condition of the utmost spiritual degradation, but enjoying the highest State patronage. The religion in favour will be one of morality, but not of dogma; and the Man of Sin will be able to promulgate his doctrine, according to S. Anselm, through his great eloquence and wisdom, his vast learning and mightiness in the Holy Scriptures, which he will wrest to the over-throwing of dogma. He will be liberal in bribes, for he will be of unbounded wealth; he will be capable of performing great 'signs and wonders', so as 'to deceive – the very elect'; and at the last, he will tear the moral veil from his countenance, and a monster of impiety and cruelty, he will inaugurate that awful persecution, which is to last for three years and a half, and to excel in horror all the persecutions that have gone before.

In that terrible season of confusion faith will be all but extinguished. 'When the Son of Man cometh shall He find faith on the earth?' asks our Blessed Lord, as though expecting the answer, No; and then, says Marchantius, the vessel of the Church will disappear in the foam of that boiling deep of infidelity, and be hidden in the blackness of that storm of destruction which sweeps over the earth. The sun shall 'be darkened, and the moon shall not give her light, and the stars shall fall from heaven'; the sun of faith shall have gone out; the moon, the Church, shall not give her light, being turned into blood, through stress of persecution; and the stars, the great ecclesiastical dignitaries, shall fall into apostasy. But still the Church will remain unwrecked, she will weather the storm; still will she come forth 'beautiful as the moon, terrible as an army with banners'; for after the lapse of those three and a half years, Christ will descend to avenge the blood of the saints, by destroying Antichrist and the world-power.

Such is a brief sketch of the Scriptural doctrine of Antichrist as held by the Early and Mediæval Church. Let us now see to what Myths it gave rise among the vulgar and the imaginative. Rabanus Maurus, in his work on the life of Antichrist, gives a full account of the miracles he will perform; he tells us that the Man-fiend will heal the sick, raise the dead, restore sight to the blind, hearing to the deaf, speech to the dumb; he will raise storms and calm them, will remove mountains, make trees flourish or wither at a word. He will rebuild the temple at Jerusalem, and make the Holy City the great capital of the world. Popular opinion added that his vast wealth would be obtained from hidden treasures, which are now being concealed by the demons for his use. Various possessed persons, when interrogated, announced that such was the case, and that the amount of buried gold was vast.

'In the year 1599,' says Canon Moreau, a contemporary historian, 'a rumour circulated with prodigious rapidity through Europe, that Antichrist had been born at Babylon, and that already the Jews of that part were hurrying to receive and recognize him as their Messiah. The news came from Italy and Germany, and extended to Spain, England, and other Western kingdoms, troubling many people, even the most discreet; however the learned gave it no credence, saying that the signs predicted in Scripture to precede that event were not yet accomplished, and among other that the Roman empire was not yet abolished. . . . Others said that, as for the signs, the majority had already appeared to the best of their knowledge, and with regard to the rest, they might have taken place in distant regions without their having been made known to them; that the Roman empire existed but in name, and that the interpretation of the passage on which its destruction was predicted, might be incorrect: that for many centuries, the most learned and pious had believed in the near approach of Antichrist, some believing that he had already come, on account of the persecutions which had fallen on the Christians; others on account of fires, or eclipses, or earthquakes. . . . Every one was in excitement; some declared that the news must be correct, others believed nothing about it, and the agitation became so excessive, that Henry IV, who was then on the throne, was compelled by edict to forbid any mention of the subject.'

The report spoken of by Moreau gained additional confirmation from the announcement made by an exorcized demoniac, that in 1600, the Man of Sin had been born in the neighbourhood of Paris of a Jewess, named Blanchefleure, who had conceived by Satan. The child had been baptized at the Sabbath of Sorcerers; and a witch, under torture, acknowledged that she had rocked the infant Antichrist on her knees, and she averred that he had claws on his feet, wore no shoes, and spoke all languages.

In 1623 appeared the following startling announcement, which obtained an immense circulation among the lower orders: 'We, brothers of the Order of S. John of Jerusalem, in the isle of Malta, have received letters from our spies, who are engaged in our service in the country of Babylon, now possessed by the Grand Turk; by the which letters we are advertised, that, on the 1st of May, in the year of our Lord 1623, a child was born in the town of Bourydot, otherwise called Calka, near Babylon, of the which child the mother is a very aged woman of race unknown, called Fort-Juda: of the father nothing is known. The child is dusky, has pleasant mouth and eyes, teeth pointed like those of a cat, ears large, stature by no means exceeding that of other children; the said child, incontinent on his birth, walked and talked perfectly well. His speech is comprehended by every one, admonishing the people that he is the true Messiah, and the son of God, and that in him all must believe. Our spies also swear and protest that they have seen the said child with their own eyes; and they add, that, on the occasion of his nativity, there appeared marvellous signs in heaven, for at full noon the sun lost its brightness, and was for some time obscured.' This is followed by a list of other signs appearing, the most remarkable being a swarm of flying serpents, and a shower of precious stones.

According to Sebastian Michaeliz, in his history of the possessed of Flanders, on the authority of the exorcized demons, we learn that Antichrist is to be a son of Beelzebub, who will accompany his offspring under the form of a bird, with four feet and a bull's head; that he will torture Christians with the same tortures with which the lost souls are racked; that he will be able to fly, speak all languages, and will have any number of names.

We find that Antichrist is known to the Mussulmans as well as to Christians. Lane, in his edition of the 'Arabian Nights', gives some curious details on Moslem ideas regarding him. According to these, Antichrist will overrun the earth, mounted on an ass, and followed by 40,000 Jews; his empire will last forty days, whereof the first day will be a year long, the duration of the second will be a month, that of the third a week, the others being of their usual length. He will devastate the whole world, leaving Mecca and Medina alone in security, as these holy cities will be guarded by angelic legions. Christ at last will descend to earth, and in a great battle will destroy the Man-devil.

Several writers of different denominations, no less superstitious than the common people, connected the apparition of Antichrist with the fable of Pope Joan, which obtained such general credence at one time, but which modern criticism has at length succeeded in excluding from history.

The earliest writer supposed to mention Pope Joan is Anastasius the Librarian, a contemporary (d. 886); next to him is Marianus Scotus, who in his chronicle inserts the following passage: 'A.D. 854, Lotharii 14, Joanna, a woman, succeeded Leo, and reigned two years, five months, and four days.' Marianus Scotus died A.D. 1086. The same story is inserted in the valuable chronicle of Sigebert de Gemblours (d. 5th Oct. 1112): 'It is reported that this John was a female, and that she conceived by one of her servants. The Pope, becoming pregnant, gave birth to a child, wherefore some do not number her among the Pontiffs.' Hence the story spread among the mediæval chroniclers, who were great plagiarists. Otto of Frisingen and Gotfrid of Viterbo mention the Lady-Pope in their histories, and Martin Polonus gives details as follows: 'After Leo IV John Anglus, a native of Metz, reigned two years, five months, and four days. And the pontificate was vacant for a month. He died in Rome. He is related to have been a female, and, when a girl, to have accompanied her sweetheart in male costume to Athens; there she advanced in various sciences, and none could be found to equal her. So, after having studied for three years in Rome, she had great masters for her pupils and hearers. And when there arose a high opinion in the city of her virtue and knowledge, she was unanimously elected Pope. But during her papacy she became in the family way by a familiar. Not knowing the time of birth, as she was on her way from S. Peter's to the Lateran she had a painful delivery, between the Coliseum and S. Clement's Church, in the street. Having died after, it is said that she was buried on the spot, and therefore the Lord Pope always turns aside from that way, and it is supposed by some, out of detestation for what happened there. Nor on that account is she placed in the catalogue of the Holy Pontiffs, not only on account of her sex, but also because of the horribleness of the circumstance.'

Certainly a story at all scandalous *crescit eundo*.

William Ocham alludes to the story, Thomas de Elmham (1422) quaintly observes, 'A.D. 855. Joannes. Iste non computatus. Fœmina fuit'; and John Huss, only too happy to believe it, provides the lady with a name, and asserts that she was baptized Agnes, or, as he will have it with a strong aspirate, Hagnes. Others, however, insist upon her name having been Gilberta, and some stout Germans, not relishing the notion of her being a daughter of Fatherland, palm her off on England. As soon as we arrive at Reformation times the German and French Protestants fasten on the story with the utmost avidity, and add sweet little touches of their own, and draw conclusions galling enough to the Roman See, illustrating their accounts with wood engravings vigorous and graphic, but hardly decent. One of these represents the event in a peculiarly startling manner. The procession of bishops with the Host and tapers is sweeping along, when suddenly the cross-bearer before the triple-crowned and vested Pope starts aside to witness the unexpected arrival. This engraving, which it is quite impossible for me to reproduce, is in a curious little book, entitled 'Puerperium Johannis Papæ 8, 1530'.

The following jingling record of the event is from the Rhythmical Vitæ Pontificum of Gulielmus Jacobus of Egmonden, a work never printed. This fragment is preserved in 'Wolffii Lectionum Memorabilium centenarii, XVI'.

> Priusquàm reconditur Sergius, vocatur
> Ad summam, qui dicitur Johannes, huic addatur
> Anglicus, Moguntia iste procreatur.
> Qui, ut dat sententia, fœminis aptatur
> Sexu: quod sequentia monstrant, breviatur,
> Hæc vox: nam prolixius chronica procedunt.
> Ista, de qua brevius dicta minus lædunt.
> Huic erat amasius, ut scriptores credunt.
> Patria relinquitur Moguntia, Græcorum
> Studiosè petitur schola. Pòst doctorum
> Hæc doctrix efficitur Romæ legens: horum
> Hæc auditu fungitur loquens. Hinc prostrato
> Summo hæc eligitur: sexu exaltato
> Quandoque negligitur. Fatur quòd hæc nato
> Per servum conficitur. Tempore gignendi
> Ad processum equus scanditur, vice flendi,
> Papa cadit, panditur improbis ridendi
> Norma, puer nascitur in vico Clementis,
> Colossœum jungitur. Corpus parentis
> In eodem traditur sepulturæ gentis,
> Faturque scriptoribus, quòd Papa præfato,
> Vico senioribus transiens amato
> Congruo ductoribus sequitur negato
> Loco, quo Ecclesia partu denigratur,
> Quamvis inter spacia Pontificum ponatur,
> Propter sexum.

Stephen Blanch, in his 'Urbis Romæ Mirabilia', says that an angel of heaven appeared to Joan before the event, and asked her to choose whether she should prefer burning eternally in hell, or having her confinement in public; with sense which does her credit, she chose the latter. The Protestant writers were not satisfied that the father of the unhappy baby should have been a servant: some made him a Cardinal, and others the devil himself. According to an eminent Dutch minister, it is immaterial whether the child be fathered on Satan or a monk: at all events, the former took a lively interest in the youthful Antichrist, and, on the occasion of his birth, was seen and heard fluttering overhead, crowing and chanting in an unmusical voice the Sibyline verses announcing the birth of the Arch-persecutor:–

> 'Papa pater patrum, Papissæ pándito partum
> Et tibi tunc eadem de corpore quando recedam!'

which lines, as being perhaps the only ones known to be of diabolic composition, are deserving of preservation.

The Reformers, in order to reconcile dates, were put to the somewhat perplexing necessity of moving Pope Joan to their own times, or else of giving to the youthful Antichrist an age of seven hundred years.

It must be allowed that the *accouchement* of a Pope in full pontificals, during a solemn procession, was a prodigy not likely to occur more than once in the world's history, and was certain to be of momentous import.

It will be seen by the curious woodcut reproduced as frontispiece from Baptista Mantuanus, that he consigned Pope Joan to the jaws of hell, notwithstanding her choice. The verses accompanying this picture are:

> Hic pendebat adhuc sexum mentita virile
> Fœmina, cui triplici Phrygiam diademate mitram
> Extollebat apex: et pontificalis adulter.

It need hardly be stated that the whole story of Pope Joan is fabulous, and rests on not the slightest historical foundation. It was probably a Greek invention to throw discredit on the papal hierarchy, first circulated more than two hundred years after the date of the supposed Pope. Even Martin Polonus (A.D. 1282), who is the first to give the details, does so merely on popular report.

The great champions of the myth were the Protestants of the sixteenth century, who were thoroughly unscrupulous in distorting history and suppressing facts, so long as they could make a point. A paper war was waged upon the subject, and finally the whole story was proved conclusively to be utterly destitute of historical truth. A melancholy example of the blindness of party feeling and prejudice is seen in Mosheim, who assumes the truth of the ridiculous story, and gravely inserts it in his 'Ecclesiastical History'. 'Between Leo IV, who died 855, and Benedict III, a woman, who concealed her sex and assumed the name of John, it is said, opened her way to the Pontifical throne by her learning and genius, and governed the Church for a time. She is commonly called the Papess Joan. During the five subsequent centuries the witnesses to this extraordinary event are without number; nor did any one, prior to the Reformation by Luther, regard the thing as either incredible or disgraceful to the Church.' Such are Mosheim's words, and I give them as a specimen of the credit which is due to his opinion. The 'Ecclesiastical History' he wrote is full of perversions of the plainest facts, and that under our notice is but one out of many. 'During the five centuries after her reign,' he says, 'the witnesses to the story are innumerable.' Now for two centuries there is not an allusion to be found to the events. The only passage which can be found is a universally acknowledged interpolation of the 'Lives of the Popes', by Anastasius Bibliothecarius, and this interpolation is stated in the first printed edition by Busæus, Mogunt, 1602, to be only found in two MS copies.

Mosheim is false again in asserting that no one prior to the Reformation regarded the thing as either incredible or disgraceful. This is but of a piece with his disregard for truth, whenever he can hit the Catholic Church hard. Bart. Platina, in his 'Lives of the Popes', written before Luther was born, after relating the story, says, 'These things which I relate are popular reports, but derived from uncertain and obscure authors, which I have therefore inserted briefly and baldly, lest I should seem to omit obstinately and pertinaciously what most people assert.' Thus the facts were justly doubted by Platina on the legitimate grounds that they rested on popular gossip, and not on reliable history. Anastasius the Librarian, contemporary of the alleged circumstance, is the first cited as evidence to there having been a Papess. This testimony is however open to serious objection. The MSS of the works of Anastasius do not uniformly contain the fable. Panvini, who wrote additions to Platina, *De vitis Romanorum Pontificum*, assures us that 'in old books of the lives of the Popes, written by Damasus, by the Librarian, and by Pandulph de Pisa, there is no mention of this woman: only on the margin, betwixt Leo IV and Benedict III, this fable has been found inserted by a later writer, in characters altogether distinct from the text.'

Blondel, the great Protestant writer, who ruined the case of the Decretals, says that he examined a MS of Anastasius in the Royal Library at Paris, and found the story of Pope Joan inserted in such a manner as to convince him that it was a late interpolation. He says, 'Having read and re-read it, I found that the elogium of the pretended Papess is taken from the words of Martinus Polonus, penitenciary to Innocent IV, and Archbishop of Cosenza, an author four hundred years later than Anastasius, and much more given to all these kinds of fables.' His reasons for so thinking are, that the style is not that of the Librarian, but similar to that of Martin Polonus; also that the insertion interferes with the text of the chronicle, and bears evidence of clumsy piecing. 'In the elogiums of Leo IV and Benedict III, as given to us in the manuscript of the Bibliothèque Royale, swelled with the romance of the Papess, the same expressions occur as in the Mayence edition; whence it follows that (according to the intention of Anastasius, violated by the rashness of those who have mingled with it their idle dreams) it is absolutely impossible that any one could have been Pope between Leo IV and Benedict III, for he says: – 'After the prelate Leo was withdrawn from this world, *at once* (mox) all the clergy, the nobles, and people of Rome hastened to elect Benedict; and at once (illico) they sought him, praying in the Titular Church of S. Callixtus, and having seating him on the pontifical throne, and signed the decree of his election, they sent him to the very-invincible Augusti Lothair and Louis, and the first of these died on 29 September, 855, just seventy-four days after the death of Pope Leo.'

Bayle in his *Dictionnaire historique et critique*, under the article Papesse Jeanne, says: 'Is it not true that if we found in a manuscript a statement that the Emperor Ferdinand II died in the year 1637, and that at once he was succeeded by Ferdinand III, and that Charles VI succeeded Ferdinand II, and held the throne for two years, after which Ferdinand III, was elected Emperor, we should say that the same writer could not have made both statements, and that we were necessitated to attribute to copyists without judgment the statements which do not correspond? Would not the man be a fool who related that Innocent X having died, he was promptly given as successor Alexander VIII, and that Innocent XI was Pope immediately after Innocent X, and sat for two years and more, and that Alexander VIII succeeded him? Anastasius Bibliothecarius must have committed a like extravagance, if he was the author of what occurs in the MSS of his work which mention the Papess. We however conclude that the statement concerning this woman was an insertion of a later hand.'

Sarran, a zealous and learned Protestant, formed the same opinion of the Pope Joan fable, and he gives as his reason for believing it not to have stood in the original copies of Anastasius, that it is there inserted with the words, 'It is said that', or 'we are assured that', expressions inconsistent with the fact that Anastasius was a contemporary resident in Rome.

Marianus Scotus, the next authority cited for the story of Pope Joan, died in 1086. He was a monk of S. Martin of Cologne, then of Fulda, and lastly, of S. Alban's, at Metz. How could he have obtained reliable information, or seen documents upon which to ground the assertion? The words in which the tale is alluded to in his Chronicle vary in different MSS, in some the fact is asserted plainly; in others, it is founded on an *ut asseritur*; and other MS copies have not the passage in them at all. This looks as though the Pope Joan passage were an interpolation. Next to Marianus Scotus comes Sigebert de Gemblours, who died 1112. We have evidence conclusive that his Chronicle has been tampered with in this particular. The Gemblours MS, which was either written by Sigebert himself, or was a copy made from his, does not allude to Pope Joan. Several other early copies have not the passage. Guillaume de Nangiac, who wrote a Chronicle to the year 1302, transcribed, and absorbed into his work, the more ancient chronicle of Sigebert. The copy used by Guillaume de Nangiac must have been without the disputed paragraph, for it is not to be found in his work. We are therefore reduced to Martin Polonus (d. 1279), placing more than four centuries between him and the event he records.

The historical discrepancies are sufficiently glaring to make the story more than questionable.

Leo IV died on the 17th July, 855; and Benedict III was consecrated on the 1st September in the same year; so that it is impossible to insert between their pontificates a reign of two years, five months, and four days. It is, however, true that there was an antipope elected upon the death of Leo, at the instance of the Emperor Louis, but his name was Anastasius. This man possessed himself of the palace of the Popes, and obtained the incarceration of Benedict. However, his supporters almost immediately deserted him, and Benedict assumed the pontificate. The reign of Benedict was only for two years and a half, so that Anastasius cannot be the supposed Joan; nor do we hear of any charge brought against him to the effect of his being a woman. But the stout partisans of the Pope Joan tale assert, on the authority of the 'Annales Augustani', and some other, but late authorities, that the female Pope was John VIII, who consecrated Louis II of France, and Ethelwolf of England. Here again is confusion. Ethelwolf sent Alfred to Rome in 853, and the youth received regal unction from the hands of Leo IV. In 855 Ethelwolf visited Rome, it is true, but was not consecrated by the existing Pope, whilst Charles the Bald was anointed by John VIII in 875. John VIII was a Roman, son of Gundus, and an archdeacon of the Eternal City. He assumed the triple crown in 872, and reigned till December 18th, 882. John took an active part in the troubles of the Church under the incursions of the Sarasins, and 325 letters of his are extant, addressed to the princes and prelates of his day.

Any one desirous of pursuing this examination into the untenable nature of the story may find an excellent summary of the arguments used on both sides in Gieseler, 'Lehrbuch', &c., Cunningham's trans., vol. ii, pp. 20, 21, or in Bayle, 'Dictionnaire', tom. iii. art. Papesse.

The arguments in favour of the myth may be seen in Spanheim, 'Exercit. de Papa Fœmina', Opp. tom. ii, p. 577, or in Lenfant, 'Histoire de la Papesse Jeanne', La Haye, 1736, 2 vols. 12mo.

The arguments on the other side may be had in 'Allatii Confutatio Fabulæ de Johanna Papissa', Colon. 1645; in Le Quien, 'Oriens Christianus', tom. iii, p. 777;

and in the pages of the Lutheran Huemann, 'Sylloge Diss. Sacras.', tom. i, par. ii, p. 352; and Blondel, 'Familier éclaircissement de la question, si une femme a été assise au siège papal de Rome', Amsterdam, 1647–9.

The final development of this extraordinary story, under the delicate fingers of the German and French Protestant controversialists, may not prove uninteresting.

Joan was the daughter of an English missionary, who left England to preach the Gospel to the recently converted Saxons. She was born at Engelheim, and according to different authors she was christened Agnes, Gerberta, Joanna, Margaret, Isabel, Dorothy, or Jutt – the last must have been a nickname surely! She early distinguished herself for genius and love of letters. A young monk of Fulda having conceived for her a violent passion, which she returned with ardour, she deserted her parents, dressed herself in male attire, and in the sacred precincts of Fulda divided her affections between the youthful monk and the musty books of the monastic library. Not satisfied with the restraints of conventual life, nor finding the library sufficiently well provided with books of abstruse science, she eloped with her young man, and after visiting England, France, and Italy, she brought him to Athens, where she addicted herself with unflagging devotion to her literary pursuits. Wearied out by his journey, the monk expired in the arms of the blue-stocking who had influenced his life for evil, and the young lady of so many aliases was for a while inconsolable. She left Athens and repaired to Rome. There she opened a school, and acquired such a reputation for learning and feigned sanctity that, on the death of Leo IV, she was unanimously elected Pope. For two years and five months, under the name of John VIII, she filled the papal chair with reputation, no one suspecting her sex. But having taken a fancy to one of the cardinals, by him she became pregnant. At length arrived the time of Rogation processions. Whilst passing the street between the amphitheatre and S. Clement's, she was seized with violent pains, fell to the ground amidst the crowd, and whilst her attendants ministered to her, was delivered of a son. Some say the child and mother died on the spot, some that she survived but was incarcerated, some that the child was spirited away to be the Antichrist of the last days. A marble monument representing the papess with her baby was erected on the spot, which was declared to be accursed to all ages.

I have little doubt myself that Pope Joan is an impersonification of the great whore of Revelation, seated on the seven hills, and is the popular expression of the idea prevalent from the twelfth to the sixteenth centuries, that the mystery of iniquity was somehow working in the papal court. The scandal of the Antipopes, the utter worldliness and pride of others, the spiritual fornication with the kings of the earth, along with the words of Revelation prophesying the advent of an adulterous woman who should rule over the imperial city, and her connexion with Antichrist, crystallized into this curious myth, much as the floating uncertainty as to the signification of our Lord's words, 'There be some standing here which shall not taste of death till they see the kingdom of God', condensed into the myth of the Wandering Jew.

The literature connected with Antichrist is voluminous. I need only specify some of the most curious works which have appeared on the subject. S. Hippolytus and Rabanus Maurus have been already alluded to. Commodianus wrote 'Carmen Apologeticum adversus Gentes', which has been published by Dom Pitra in his 'Spicilegium Solesmense', with an introduction containing Jewish and Christian traditions relating to Antichrist. 'De Turpissima Conceptione, Nativitate, et aliis Præsagiis Diaboliciis illius Turpissimi Hominis Antichrist', is the title of a strange little volume published by Lenoir in A.D. 1500, containing rude yet characteristic woodcuts, representing the birth, life, and death of the Man of Sin, each picture accompanied by French verses in explanation. An equally remarkable illustrated work on Antichrist is the famous 'Liber de Antichristo', a blockbook of an early date. It is in twenty-seven folios, and is excessively rare. Dibdin has reproduced three of the plates in his 'Bibliotheca Spenseriana', and Falckenstein has given full details of the work in his 'Geschichte der Buchdruckerkunst'.

There is an Easter miracle-play of the twelfth century, still extant, the subject of which is the 'Life and Death of Antichrist'. More curious still is the 'Farce de l'Antéchrist et de trois femmes', a composition of the sixteenth century, when that mysterious personage occupied all brains. The farce consists in a scene at a fish-stall, with three good ladies quarrelling over some fish. Antichrist steps in – for no particular reason that one can see – upsets fish and fish-women, sets them fighting, and skips off the stage. The best book on Antichrist, and that most full of learning and judgment, is Malvenda's great work in two folio volumes, 'De Antichristo, libri xii', Lyons, 1647.

For the fable of the Pope Joan, see J. Lenfant, 'Histoire de la Papesse Jeanne', La Haye, 1736, 2 vols. 12mo; 'Allatii Confutatio Fabulæ de Johanna Papissa', Colon, 1645.

CHAPTER 5

The Man in the Moon

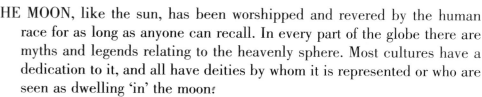

THE MOON, like the sun, has been worshipped and revered by the human race for as long as anyone can recall. In every part of the globe there are myths and legends relating to the heavenly sphere. Most cultures have a dedication to it, and all have deities by whom it is represented or who are seen as dwelling 'in' the moon.

In Greece the Goddess Selene (or sometimes Artemis) ruled the moon; in China Kwan Yin; in South America the Myan Ixchel or the Inca Mamaquilla (Mother Moon). Egypt saw the face in the moon as representing Thoth, although the moon was also the left eye of Horus. The Babylonian moon god, Sin, was the regulator of human life, while in Carthage the virgin Queen Tanit was represented by the moon. In Central Asia the moon was known as the Old Man and was seen as a great mirror which reflected back the actions of mankind, revealing both its good and its bad side.

In Cambodia the face is seen as belonging to Pajan Yan, goddess of healing, who was banished from earth before she could give eternal life to the dead and thus upset the order of Creation. In China the inhabitant of the moon whose face one may see is Ch'ang O, who stole the Elixir of Life and was transformed into a three-legged toad as punishment. Among the Esquimaux the story is told that the moon (here masculine) crept into bed with his sister the sun and attempted to rape her. In retaliation she marked his face with ashes and ever since has pursued him through the sky. As well as the figures mentioned by Gould, Western traditions place Cain, Endymion and Judas in the moon. Buddhist tradition says that Buddha, in one of his early incarnations, offered himself as a hare to be sacrificed to the god Sakra, who painted the hare on the moon as a memorial of this deed. In New Guinea the pattern of marks represent some mischievous boys who opened a jar in which the Old Woman kept the moon. As it rose into the sky they were pulled up with it and are there to this day.

Also in Greek myth there was a terrifying apparition in the moon which scared away the impious. The great Roman essayist Plutarch wrote a dialogue in which this was discussed at length. It seems to have been a fable devised to discourage suicide, which was believed to take place most often by moonlight and which, in Greece as elsewhere, was unlawful.

Although the moon is now generally thought of as female, this was not always so. In almost every tradition the world over the moon was – and in many cases still is – thought of as male. Thus the idea of the Man in the Moon may well preserve a much older tradition than has been recognized.

In Peru the moon *was* always female and was called 'the wife of the sun'. One writer, Garcilaso de la Vega (1539–1616), describes a lunar temple, the walls of which were lined with polished silver 'so that their whiteness might immediately proclaim the chamber of the moon'. His description continues: 'as in the case of the sun, this temple contained a likeness of the moon, portrayed as a woman's face formed and drawn on a great silver ingot'.

In our own time the moon has lost none of its fascination, despite the fact that human feet have walked on the face of the Man in the Moon himself (one wonders what Gould would have made of this fact). Now speculation is more concerned with the shapes and patterns to be discerned on the lunar surface with the help of modern telescopes and satellite pictures; and the shapes are deemed to be those of abandoned lunar cities belonging to some ancient race of alien beings – not such a far cry as all that from the speculations of our ancestors.

Nor should we forget another contribution to folklore, from the pen of the great fantasist J. R. R. Tolkien who extracts a new and expanded version of the old nursery rhyme and puts it into the mouth of his hero Bilbo Baggins in the monumental *Lord of the Rings*.

*   *   *

EVERY one knows that the moon is inhabited by a man with a bundle of sticks on his back, who has been exiled thither for many centuries, and who is so far off that he is beyond the reach of Death.

He has once visited this earth, if the nursery rhyme is to be credited, when it asserts that –

> The Man in the Moon
> Came down too soon,
> And asked his way to Norwich;

but whether he ever reached that city, the same authority does not state.

The story as told by nurses is, that this man was found by Moses gathering sticks on a Sabbath, and that, for this crime, he was doomed to reside in the moon till the end of all things; and they refer to Numbers xv, 32–36:

'And while the children of Israel were in the wilderness, they found a man that gathered sticks upon the sabbath day. And they that found him gathering sticks brought him unto Moses and Aaron, and unto all the congregation. And they put him in ward, because it was not declared what should be done to him. And the Lord said unto Moses, The man shall be surely put to death: all the congregation shall stone him with stones without the camp. And all the congregation brought him without the camp, and stoned him with stones till he died.'

Of course, in the sacred writings there is no allusion to the moon.

The German tale is as follows:—

Ages ago there went one Sunday morning an old man into the wood to hew sticks. He cut a faggot and slung it on a stout staff, cast it over his shoulder, and began to trudge home with his burden. On his way he met a handsome man in Sunday suit, walking towards the Church; this man stopped and asked the faggot-bearer, 'Do you know that this is Sunday on earth, when all must rest from their labours?'

'Sunday on earth, or Monday in heaven, it is all one to me!' laughed the wood-cutter.

'Then bear your bundle for ever,' answered the stranger; 'and as you value not Sunday on earth, yours shall be a perpetual Moon-day in heaven; and you shall stand for eternity in the moon, a warning to all Sabbath-breakers.' Thereupon the stranger vanished, and the man was caught up with his stock and his faggot into the moon, where he stands yet.

The superstition seems to be old in Germany, for the full moon is spoken of as *wadel*, or *wedel*, a faggot. Tobler relates the story thus: 'An arma ma ket alawel am Sonnti holz ufglesa. Do hedem der liebe Gott dwahl gloh, öb er lieber wött ider sonn verbrenna oder im mo verfrüra, do willer lieber inn mo ihi. Dromm siedma no jetz an ma im mo inna, wenns wedel ist. Er hed a püscheli uffem rogga.' That is to say, he was given the choice of burning in the sun, or of freezing in the moon; he chose the latter; and now at full moon he is to be seen seated with his bundle of faggots on his back.

In Schaumburg-lippe, the story goes, that a man and a woman stand in the moon, the man because he strewed brambles and thorns on the church path, so as to hinder people from attending Mass on Sunday morning; the woman because she made butter on that day. The man carries his bundle of thorns, the woman her butter-tub. A similar tale is told in Swabia and in Marken. Fischart says that there 'is to be seen in the moon a mannikin who stole wood', and Prætorius, in his description of the world, that 'superstitious people assert that the black flecks in the moon are a man who gathered wood on a Sabbath, and is therefore turned into stone'.

At the time when wishing was of avail, say the North Frisians, a man, one Christmas eve, stole cabbages from his neighbour's garden. When just in the act of walking off with his load, he was perceived by the people, who conjured him up into the moon. There he stands in the full moon to be seen by every body, bearing his load of cabbages to all eternity. Every Christmas eve he is said to turn round once. Others say that he stole willow bows, which he must bear for ever.

In Silt, the story goes that he was a sheep-stealer, who enticed sheep to him with a bundle of cabbages, until, as an everlasting warning to others, he was placed in the moon, where he constantly holds in his hand a bundle of these vegetables.

The people of Rantum say that he is a giant, who at the time of the flow stands in a stooping posture, because he is then taking up water, which he pours out on the earth, and thereby causes high tide; but at the time of the ebb he stands erect, and rests from his labour, when the water can subside again.

The Dutch household myth is, that the unhappy man was caught stealing vegetables. Dante calls him Cain:–

> . . . Now doth Cain with fork of thorns confine,
> On either hemisphere, touching the wave
> Beneath the towers of Seville. Yesternight
> The moon was round. – *Hell*, cant. xx.

And again,

> . . . Tell, I pray thee, whence the gloomy spots
> Upon this body, which below on earth
> Give rise to talk of Cain in fabling quaint?
> *Paradise*, cant. ii.

Chaucer, in the 'Testament of Cresside', adverts to the man in the moon, and attributes to him the same idea of theft. Of Lady Cynthia, or the moon, he says: –

> Her gite was gray and full of spottis blake,
> And on her brest a chorle painted ful even,
> Bering a bush of thornis on his backe,
> Whiche for his theft might clime so ner the heaven.

Ritson, among his 'Ancient Songs', gives one extracted from a manuscript attributed by Mr Wright to the period of Edward I, on the Man in the Moon; but in very obscure language. The first verse, altered into more modern orthography, runs as follows:–

> Man in the Moon stand and stit,
>   On his bot-fork his burden he beareth,
> It is much wonder that he do na doun slit,
>   For doubt lest he fall he shudd'reth and shivereth.
>
> When the frost freezes must chill he bide,
>   The thorns be keen his attire so teareth,
> Nis no wight in the world there wot when he syt,
>   Ne bote it by the hedge what weeds he weareth.

Alexander Necham, or Nequam, a writer of the twelfth century, in commenting on the dispersed shadows in the moon, thus alludes to the vulgar belief:– 'Nonne novisti quid vulgus vocet rusticum in luna portantem spinas? Unde quidam vulgariter loquens ait:–

> "Rusticus in Luna,
> Quem sarcina deprimit una
> Monstrat per opinas
> Nulli prodesse rapinas," '

51

which may be translated thus: 'Do you know what they call the rustic in the moon, who carries the faggot of sticks? So that one vulgarly speaking says:–

> "See the rustic in the Moon,
> How his bundle weighs him down;
> Thus his sticks the truth reveal,
> It never profits man to steal." '

Shakspeare refers to the same individual in his 'Midsummer Night's Dream'. Quince the carpenter, giving directions for the performance of the play of 'Pyramus and Thisbe', orders: 'One must come in with a bush of thorns and a lantern, and say he comes in to disfigure, or to present, the person of Moonshine.' And the enacter of this part says, 'All I have to say is, to tell you that the lantern is the moon; I the man in the moon; this thorn-bush my thorn-bush; and this dog my dog.'

Also 'Tempest', Act 2, Scene 2:–

Cal.   Hast thou not dropt from heav'n?
Steph. Out o' th' moon, I do assure thee. I was the man in th' moon when time was.
Cal.   I have seen thee in her; and I do adore thee. My mistress show'd me thee, and thy dog, and thy bush.

The dog I have myself had pointed out to me by an old Devonshire crone. If popular superstition places a dog in the moon, it puts a lamb in the sun; for in the same county it is said that those who see the sun rise on Easter-day may behold in the orb the lamb and flag.

I believe this idea of locating animals in the two great luminaries of heaven to be very ancient, and to be a relic of a primeval superstition of the Aryan race.

There is an ancient pictorial representation of our friend the Sabbath-breaker in Gyffyn Church, near Conway. The roof of the chancel is divided into compartments, in four of which are the Evangelistic symbols, rudely, yet effectively painted. Besides these symbols is delineated in each compartment an orb of heaven. The sun, the moon, and two stars, are placed at the feet of the Angel, the Bull, the Lion, and the Eagle. The representation of the moon . . . in the disk is the conventional man with his bundle of sticks, but without the dog. There is also a curious seal appended to a deed preserved in the Record Office, dated the 9th year of Edward the Third (1335), bearing the man in the moon as its device. The deed is one of conveyance of a messuage, barn, and four acres of ground, in the parish of Kingston-on-Thames, from Walter de Grendesse, clerk, to Margaret his mother. On the seal we see the man carrying his sticks, and the moon surrounds him. There are also a couple of stars added, perhaps to show that he is in the sky. The legend on the seal reads:–

> Te Waltere docebo
> cur spinas phebo
> gero,

which may be translated, 'I will teach thee, Walter, why I carry thorns in the moon.'

The carved wooden sign of the 'Man in the Moon', in Wych Street, Strand, a rare example of the suspended signs now to be found built into the wall, must not pass unnoticed. Other items connected with lunar mythology must be only briefly alluded to. According to the classic tale the figure in the moon is probably Endymion, beloved of Selene, and held by her passionately to her bosom. The Egyptian representations of the moon with a figure in the disk, represent the little Horus in the womb of his mother Isis. Plutarch wrote a tract on the Face in the Moon. Clemens Alexandrinus tells us the face is that of a Sibyl.

The general superstition with regard to the spots in the moon may briefly be summed up thus: A man is located in the moon; he is a thief or Sabbath-breaker; he has a pole over his shoulder, from which is suspended a bundle of sticks or thorns. In some places a woman is believed to accompany him, and she has a butter-tub with her; in other localities she is replaced by a dog.

The belief in the Moon-man seems to exist among the natives of British Columbia; for I read in one of Mr Duncan's letters to the Church Missionary Society:– 'One very dark night I was told that there was a moon to see on the beach. On going to see, there was an illuminated disk, with the figure of a man upon it. The water was then very low, and one of the conjuring parties had lit up this disk at the water's edge. They had made it of wax with great exactness, and presently it was at full. It was an imposing sight. Nothing could be seen around it; but the Indians suppose that the medicine party are then holding converse with the man in the moon. . . . After a short time the moon waned away, and the conjuring party returned whooping to their house.'

Now let us turn to Scandinavian mythology, and see what we learn from that source.

Mâni, the moon, stole two children from their parents, and carried them up to heaven. Their names were Hjuki and Bil. They had been drawing water from the well Byrgir, in the bucket Sœgr, suspended from the pole Simul, which they bore upon their shoulders. These children, pole, and bucket, were placed in heaven, 'where they could be seen from earth'. This refers undoubtedly to the spots in the moon, and so the Swedish peasantry explain these spots to this day, as representing a boy and a girl bearing a pail of water between them. Are we not reminded at once of our nursery rhyme–

> Jack and Jill went up a hill
> To fetch a pail of water;
> Jack fell down, and broke his crown,
> And Jill came tumbling after?

This verse, which to us seems at first sight nonsense, I have no hesitation in saying has a high antiquity, and refers to the Eddaic Hjuki and Bil. The names indicate as much. Hjuki, in Norse, would be pronounced Juki, which would readily become Jack; and Bil, for the sake of euphony, and in order to give a female name to one of the children, would become Jill.

The fall of Jack, and the subsequent fall of Jill, simply represent the vanishing of one moon-spot after another, as the moon wanes.

But the old Norse myth had a deeper signification than merely an explanation of the moon-spots.

Hjuki is derived from the verb jakka, to heap or pile together, to assemble and increase; and Bil from bila, to break up or dissolve. Hjuki and Bil, therefore, signify nothing more than the waxing and waning of the moon, and the water they are represented as bearing signifies the fact that the rainfall depends on the phases of the moon. Waxing and waning were individualized, and the meteorological fact of the connexion of the rain with the moon was represented by the children as water-bearers.

But though Jack and Jill became by degrees dissevered in the popular mind from the moon, the original myth went through a fresh phase, and exists still under a new form. The Norse superstition attributed *theft* to the moon and the vulgar soon began to believe that the figure they saw in the moon was the thief. The lunar specks certainly may be made to resemble one figure, but only a lively imagination can discern two. The girl soon dropped out of popular mythology, the boy oldened into a venerable man, he retained his pole, and the bucket was transformed into the thing he had stolen – sticks or vegetables. The theft was in some places exchanged for Sabbath-breaking, especially among those in Protestant countries who were acquainted with the Bible story of the stick-gatherer.

The Indian superstition is worth examining, because of the connexion existing between Indian and European mythology, on account of our belonging to the same Aryan stock.

According to a Buddhist legend, Sâkyamunni himself, in one of his earlier stages of existence, was a hare, and lived in friendship with a fox and an ape. In order to test the virtue of the Bodhisattwa, Indra came to the friends, in the form of an old man asking for food. Hare, ape, and fox went forth in quest of victuals for their guest. The two latter returned from their foraging expedition successful, but the hare had found nothing. Then, rather than that he should treat the old man with inhospitality, the hare had a fire kindled, and cast himself into the flames, that he might himself become food for his guest. In reward for this act of self-sacrifice, Indra carried the hare to heaven, and placed him in the moon.

Here we have an old man and a hare in connexion with the lunar planet, just as in Shakspeare we have a faggot-bearer and a dog.

The fable rests upon the name of the moon in Sanskrit, çaçin, or 'that marked with the hare'; but whether the belief in the spots taking the shape of a hare gave the name çaçin to the moon, or the lunar name çaçin originated the belief, it is impossible for us to say.

Grounded upon this myth is the curious story of 'The Hare and the Elephant', in the 'Pantschatantra', an ancient collection of Sanskrit fables. It will be found as the first tale in the third book. I have room only for an outline of the story.

THE CRAFTY HARE.

In a certain forest lived a mighty elephant, king of a herd, Toothy by name. On a certain occasion there was a long drought, so that pools, tanks, swamps, and lakes were dried up. Then the elephants sent out exploring parties in search of water. A young one discovered an extensive lake surrounded with trees, and teeming with water-fowl. It went by the name of the Moon-lake. The elephants, delighted at the prospect of having an inexhaustible supply of water, marched off to the spot, and found their most sanguine hopes realized. Round about the lake, in the sandy soil, were innumerable hare warrens, and as the herd of elephants trampled on the ground, the hares were severely injured, their homes broken down, their heads, legs, and backs crushed beneath the ponderous feet of the monsters of the forest. As soon as the herd had withdrawn, the hares assembled, some halting, some dripping with blood, some bearing the corpses of their cherished infants, some with piteous tales of ruination in their houses, all with tears streaming from their eyes, and wailing forth, 'Alas, we are lost! The elephant-herd will return, for there is no water elsewhere, and that will be the death of all of us.'

But the wise and prudent Longear volunteered to drive the herd away, and he succeeded in this manner: Longear went to the elephants, and having singled out their king, he addressed him as follows:–

'Ha, ha! bad elephant! what brings you with such thoughtless frivolity to this strange lake? back with you at once!'

When the king of the elephants heard this, he asked in astonishment, 'Pray who are you?'

'I,' replied Longear, 'I am Vidschajadatta by name, the hare who resides in the Moon. Now am I sent by his Excellency the Moon as an ambassador to you. I speak to you in the name of the Moon.'

'Ahem! Hare,' said the elephant, somewhat staggered, 'and what message have you brought me from his Excellency the Moon?'

'You have this day injured several hares. Are you not aware that they are the subjects of me? If you value your life, venture not near the lake again. Break my command, and I shall withdraw my beams from you at night, and your bodies will be consumed with perpetual sun.'

The elephant after a short meditation said, 'Friend! it is true that I have acted against the rights of the excellent Majesty of the Moon. I should wish to make an apology; how can I do so?'

The hare replied, 'Come along with me, and I will show you.'

The elephant asked, 'Where is his Excellency at present?'

The other replied, 'He is now in the lake, hearing the complaints of the maimed hares.'

'If that be the case,' said the elephant humbly, 'bring me to my lord, that I may tender him my submission.'

So the hare conducted the king of the elephants to the edge of the lake, and showed him the reflexion of the moon in the water, saying, 'There stands our lord in the midst of the water, plunged in meditation; reverence him with devotion, and then depart with speed.'

Thereupon the elephant poked his proboscis into the water, and muttered a fervent prayer. By so doing he set the water in agitation, so that the reflection of the moon was all of a quiver.

'Look!' exclaimed the hare, 'his Majesty is trembling with rage at you!'

'Why is his supreme Excellency enraged with me?' asked the elephant.

'Because you have set the water in motion. Worship him, and then be off!'

The elephant let his ears droop, bowed his great head to the earth, and after having expressed in suitable terms his regret for having annoyed the Moon and the hare dwelling in it, he vowed never to trouble the Moon-lake again. Then he departed, and the hares have ever since lived there unmolested.

CHAPTER 6

The Mountain of Venus

ALMOST EVERY mythology in the world has its tale of the mountain which holds up the sky, which is the navel of the world, and is the home of faery people, dwarfs, giants, dragons or gods, which has its own mirror-world within, where trees and flowers grow, rivers run, and stars shine out from the hidden vaults of the roof.

Mountains were, of their very nature, mysterious. They stretched upwards towards the empyrean heights and were the dwelling-places of the gods. From Mount Olympus in Greece to Muntsalvache in the Pyrenees and Valhalla in the lands of the North, all are the abode of wondrous beings, strange events and lost and wandering souls who eternally seek the divine 'other' within the vast hearts of these mighty peaks.

Among the Navaho people of Native America the night chants depict a nocturnal masque of the hero's ascent to the upper world, aided by Spider Woman who helps him to defeat his enemies and as a reward is given the sacred mountain chant, designed to bring physical and spiritual blessings.

Gould is hesitant to suggest a meaning for the primal story on which the various versions of the Venusberg myth are based. However, it is not so hard to see, in the countless tales of mortals carried away into the world of Faery, a longing for the undying beauty of the Otherworld, a place where everything is more real, and where joy and plenty overflow. Gould, of course, as a Christian priest could not really embrace these ideas – though the longing for Heaven is just as much a part of this innate human desire for peace and eternal happiness. Thus he degrades the story, which in its original form is one of great beauty, reflecting deeply upon the human condition.

Other than in her classical guise, as the Goddess of Love, Venus herself appears in many forms throughout the later literature of the West. She makes a notable appearance in the mystical text of *The Chymical Wedding of Christian Rosencreutz* (1616)

57

where the mysterious hero C.R., having dressed in wedding clothes, enters the Rosicrucian Vault and finds himself in the presence of the naked Venus. He becomes her servant and lives in the joy of her presence. The Venus of this story is both the goddess of classical times and the Otherworldly Mistress of the Faery Lands. C.R. is like Thomas of Ercildoune and Tam Lin, both of whom are taken into the Otherworld by its reigning Queen and become her consorts for a year and a day – often denoting the passage of a far greater time-span.

The Venus of the Tannhäuser legends is more like the Scandinavian Holda or Freia (as Gould notes). Tannhäuser means 'forest dweller' and may well derive from Wotanhäuser, the mountain where Freia and Woytan lived. And in the fifteenth-century poem 'Die Morin' by Herman von Sachsenheim, we hear of a later hero who travels to the realm of Faery and there encounters Queen Venus and King Tannhäuser – the latter having replaced the original inhabitants of the mountain.

Sachsenheim's description of the Venusberg has been seen to preserve vestiges of a far older myth and, as the following quotation shows, offers a suggestion as to the original inhabitant of the Mountain of Venus:

> Before the tent a grey-haired man,
> His beard was long and fair to see,
> As though that Ekkehart was he
> In Venus Hill who doth abide;
> A tiny dwarf stood by his side . . .
> The old man grinned and rubbed his beard.
> 'Now tell, dear dwarf, for 'tis my will,
> How come we in Dame Venus' Hill? . . .
> The scribe he was right good of heart
> And told us much most strange to hear
> The country's wonders far and near,
> How in the Venus Mount there stayed
> Both dames and knights and dwarf and maid.
> In many sports they while the time,
> With harp and song and ancient rhyme,
> And horns and pipes in great array . . .
>
> (translated by P. S. Barto)

Eckhart is well known in German folklore as an old man who goes ahead of the procession led by Frau Holle, a sublimated goddess-figure who captures the souls of the departed in a manner reminiscent of the native British Wild Hunt. Meeting him in this context suggests that he may be the original consort or servant of Dame Venus.

Tannhäuser himself was in fact a real figure, a thirteenth-century minnesinger or wandering bard. His legendary journeys throughout Germany and his crusade to the Holy Land seem to have led him to be identified with a mythical Tannhäuser, or with the older figure of Eckhart, certainly dating back further than the fourteenth-century stories featuring the visit to the Venusberg. Richard Wagner's powerful operatic treatment (1845) is still the form in which the story is best known today, and he adds significantly to it.

In Wagner's version the hero returns from Venusberg to the court of the Landgrave of Thuringia, where his love Elizabeth has been faithfully awaiting him. His friend Wolfram von Eschenbach persuades him to take part in a famous song contest, of which the winner will marry Elizabeth. Tannhäuser breaks into a song in praise of Venus, so wildly pagan in content that the other contestants threaten to kill him. Elizabeth begs for his life and he is released to visit the Pope and ask for forgiveness. As in the original story this is refused and Tannhäuser returns weakened and dejected, in time to see Elizabeth, who has died broken-hearted, laid to rest. Her lover falls dead upon her bier just as messengers from Rome appear with news of the miracle and the Pope's absolution.

The story has haunted the imagination of more contemporary writers, such as Thomas Mann whose famous novel *The Magic Mountain* is filled with echoes of the Tannhäuser myth and Aubrey Beardsley whose highly charged novel, *The Mount of Venus*, devotes most of its length to describing the erotic pursuits of its hero. A sequel to the story of Tannhäuser appears in the tale of Lohengrin, which will be discussed in the introduction to a later chapter, 'The Knight of the Swan'.

*   *   *

RAGGED, bald, and desolate, as though a curse rested upon it, rises the Hörselberg out of the rich and populous land between Eisenach and Gotha, looking, from a distance, like a huge stone sarcophagus – a sarcophagus in which rests in magical slumber, till the end of all things, a mysterious world of wonders.

High up on the north-west flank of the mountain, in a precipitous wall of rock, opens a cavern, called the Hörselloch, from the depths of which issues a muffled roar of water, as though a subterraneous stream were rushing over rapidly-whirling mill-wheels. 'When I have stood alone on the ridge of the mountain,' says Bechstein, 'after having sought the chasm in vain, I have heard a mighty rush, like that of falling water, beneath my feet, and after scrambling down the scarp, have found myself – how, I never knew – in front of the cave.'

In ancient days, according to the Thüringian Chronicles, bitter cries and long-drawn moans were heard issuing from this cavern; and at night wild shrieks, and the burst of diabolical laughter would ring out from it over the vale, and fill the inhabitants with terror. It was supposed that this hole gave admittance to Purgatory; and the popular but faulty derivation of Hörsel was *Hore, die Seele*, Hark, the Souls!

But another popular belief respecting this mountain was, that in it Venus, the pagan Goddess of Love, held her court in all the pomp and revelry of heathendom; and there were not a few who declared that they had seen fair forms of female beauty beckoning them from the mouth of the chasm, and that they had heard dulcet strains of music well up from the abyss above the thunder of the falling, unseen torrent. Charmed by the music, and allured by the spectral forms, various individuals had entered the cave, and none had returned except the Tanhäuser, of whom more anon. Still does the Hörselberg go by the name of the Venusberg, a name frequently used in the Middle Ages, but without its locality being always defined.

'In 1398, at mid-day, there appeared suddenly three great fires in the air, which presently ran together into one globe of flame, parted again and finally sank into the Hörselberg,' says the Thüringian Chronicle.

And now for the story of Tanhäuser.

A French knight was riding over the beauteous meadows in the Hörsel vale on his way to Wartburg, where the Landgrave Hermann was holding a gathering of minstrels, who were to contend in song for a prize.

Tanhäuser was a famous minnesinger, and all his lays were of love and of women, for his heart was full of passion, and that not of the purest and noblest description.

It was towards dusk that he passed the cliff in which is the Hörselloch, and as he rode by, he saw a white glimmering figure of matchless beauty standing before him, and beckoning him to her. He knew her at once, by her attributes and by her super-human perfection, to be none other than Venus. As she spake to him the sweetest strains of music floated in the air, a soft roseate light glowed around her, and nymphs of exquisite loveliness scattered roses at her feet. A thrill of passion ran through the veins of the minnesinger; and, leaving his horse, he followed the apparition. It led him up the mountain to the cave, and as it went flowers bloomed upon the soil, and a radiant track was left for Tanhäuser to follow. He entered the cavern, and descended to the palace of Venus in the heart of the mountain.

Seven years of revelry and debauch were passed, and the minstrel's heart began to feel a strange void. The beauty, the magnificence, the variety, of the scenes in the pagan goddess's home, and all its heathenish pleasures, palled upon him, and he yearned for the pure fresh breezes of earth, one look up at the dark night sky spangled with stars, one glimpse of simple mountain flowers, one tinkle of sheep-bells. At the same time his conscience began to reproach him, and he longed to make his peace with God. In vain did he entreat Venus to permit him to depart, and it was only when in the bitterness of his grief he called upon the Virgin-Mother, that a rift in the mountain-side appeared to him, and he stood again above ground.

How sweet was the morning air, balmy with the scent of hay, as it rolled up the mountain to him, and fanned his haggard cheek! How delightful to him was the cushion of moss and scanty grass after the downy couches of the palace of revelry below! He plucked the little heather-bells and held them before him; the tears rolled from his eyes, and moistened his thin and wasted hands. He looked up at the soft blue sky and the newly-risen sun, and his heart overflowed. What were the golden jewel-incrusted, lamp-lit vaults beneath to that pure dome of God's building!

The chime of a village church struck sweetly on his ear, satiated with Bacchanalian songs; and he hurried down the mountain to the church which called him. There he made his confession, but the priest, horror-struck at his recital, dared not give him absolution, but passed him on to another. And so he went from one to another, till at last he was referred to the Pope himself. To the Pope he went. Urban IV then occupied the chair of S. Peter. To him Tanhäuser related the sickening story of his guilt, and prayed for absolution. Urban was a hard and stern man, and shocked at the immensity of the sin, he thrust the penitent indignantly from him, exclaiming, 'Guilt such as thine can never, never be remitted. Sooner shall this staff in my hand grow green and blossom, than that God should pardon thee!'

Then Tanhäuser, full of despair, and with his soul darkened, went away, and returned to the only asylum open to him, the Venusberg. But lo! three days after he had gone, Urban discovered that his pastoral staff had put forth buds, and had burst into flower. Then he sent messengers after Tanhäuser, and they reached the Hörsel vale to hear that a wayworn man, with haggard brow and bowed head, had just entered the Hörselloch. Since then the Tanhäuser has not been seen.

Such is the sad yet beautiful story of Tanhäuser. It is a very ancient myth Christianized, a widespread tradition localized. Originally heathen, it has been transformed, and has acquired new beauty by an infusion of Christianity. Scattered over Europe, it exists in various forms, but in none so graceful as that attached to the Hörselberg. There are, however, other Venusbergs in Germany: as, for instance, in Swabia, near Waldsee; another near Ufhausen, at no great distance from Freiburg (the same story is told of this Venusberg as of the Hörselberg); in Saxony there is a Venusberg not far from Wolkenstein. Paracelsus speaks of a Venusberg in Italy, referring to that in which Æneas Sylvius says Venus or a Sibyl resides, occupying a cavern, and assuming once a week the form of a serpent. Geiler v. Keysersperg, a quaint old preacher of the fifteenth century, speaks of the witches assembling on the Venusberg, but does not say where it is.

The story, either in prose or verse, has often been printed. Some of the earliest editions are the following:–

'Das Lied von dem Danhewser', Nürnberg, without date; the same, Nürnberg, 1515. – 'Das Lyedt v. d. Thanheuser', Leyptzk, 1520. – 'Das Lied v. d. Danheüser', reprinted by Bechstein, 1835. – 'Das Lied vom edlen Tanheuser, Mons Veneris', Frankfort, 1614; Leipzig, 1668. – 'Twe lede volgen Dat erste vam Danhüsser'. Without date. – 'Van heer Danielken', Tantwerpen, 1544. – A Danish version in 'Nyerup Danske Viser', No. VIII.

Let us now see some of the forms which this remarkable myth assumed in other countries. Every popular tale has its root, a root which may be traced among different countries, and though the accidents of the story may vary, yet the substance remains unaltered. It has been said that the common people never invent new story-radicals any more than we invent new word-roots, and this is perfectly true. The same story-root remains, but it is varied according to the temperament of the narrator or the exigencies of localization. The story-root of the Venusberg is this:–

The underground folk seek union with human beings.

α. A man is enticed into their abode, where he unites with a woman of the underground race.

β. He desires to revisit the earth, and escapes.

γ. He returns again to the region below.

Now there is scarcely a collection of folk-lore which does not contain a story founded on this root. It appears in every branch of the Aryan family, and examples might be quoted from Modern Greek, Albanian, Neapolitan, French, German, Danish, Norwegian and Swedish, Icelandic, Scotch, Welsh, and other collections of popular tales. I have only space to mention some.

There is a Norse Thattr of a certain Helgi Thorir's son, which is, in its present form, a production of the fourteenth century. Helgi and his brother Thorstein went a cruise to Finnmark, or Lapland. They reached a ness, and found the land covered with forest. Helgi explored this forest, and lighted suddenly on a party of red-dressed women riding upon red horses. These ladies were beautiful and of Troll race. One surpassed the others in beauty, and she was their mistress. They erected a tent and prepared a feast. Helgi observed that all their vessels were of silver and gold. The lady, who named herself Ingibjorg, advanced towards the Norseman, and invited him to live with her. He feasted and lived with the Trolls for three days, and then returned to his ship, bringing with him two chests of silver and gold, which Ingibjorg had given him. He had been forbidden to mention where he had been and with whom, so he told no one whence he had obtained the chests. The ships sailed, and he returned home.

One winter's night Helgi was fetched away from home, in the midst of a furious storm, by two mysterious horsemen, and no one was able to ascertain for many years what had become of him, till the prayers of the king, Olaf, obtained his release, and then he was restored to his father and brother, but he was thenceforth blind. All the time of his absence he had been with the red-vested lady in her mysterious abode of Glœsisvellir.

The Scotch story of Thomas of Ercildoune is the same story. Thomas met with a strange lady, of elfin race, beneath Eildon Tree, who led him into the underground land, where he remained with her for seven years. He then returned to earth, still, however, remaining bound to come to his royal mistress whenever she should summon him. Accordingly, while Thomas was making merry with his friends in the Tower of Ercildoune, a person came running in, and told, with marks of fear and astonishment, that a hart and a hind had left the neighbouring forest, and were parading the street of the village. Thomas instantly arose, left his house, and followed the animals into the forest, from which he never returned. According to popular belief, he still 'drees his weird' in Fairy Land, and is one day expected to revisit earth (Scott, 'Minstrelsy of the Scottish Border'). Compare with this the ancient ballad of Tamlane.

Debes relates that 'it happened a good while since, when the burghers of Bergen had the commerce of the Faroe Isles, that there was a man in Serraade, called Jonas Soideman, who was kept by the spirits in a mountain during the space of seven years, and at length came out, but lived afterwards in great distress and fear, lest they should again take him away; wherefore people were obliged to watch him in the night.' The same author mentions another young man who had been carried away, and after his return was removed a second time, upon the eve of his marriage.

Gervase of Tilbury says that 'in Catalonia there is a lofty mountain, named Cavagum, at the foot of which runs a river with golden sands, in the vicinity of which there are likewise silver mines. This mountain is steep, and almost inaccessible. On its top, which is always covered with ice and snow, is a black and bottomless lake, into which if a stone be cast, a tempest suddenly arises; and near this lake is the portal of the palace of demons.' He then tells how a young damsel was spirited in there and spent seven years with the mountain spirits. On her return to earth she was thin and withered, with wandering eyes, and almost bereft of understanding.

A Swedish story is to this effect. A young man was on his way to his bride, when he was allured into a mountain by a beautiful elfin woman. With her he lived forty years, which passed as an hour; on his return to earth all his old friends and relations were dead, or had forgotten him, and finding no rest there, he returned to his mountain elf-land.

In Pomerania, a labourer's son, John Dietrich of Rambin, is said to have spent twelve years in the underground land. When about eight years old he was sent to spend a summer with his uncle, a farmer in Rodenkirchen. Here John had to keep cows with other boys, and they used to drive them to graze about the Nine-hills. There was an old cowherd, Klas Starkwolt, who used to join the boys, and tell them stories of the underground people who dwelt in a glorious land beneath the Nine-hills. These tales John swallowed eagerly, and could think of little else. One Midsummer day he ran to the hills, and laid himself down on the top of one of them, where, according to Klas, the little people were wont to dance. John lay quite still from ten till twelve at night. At last a distant tower-clock tolled midnight. Instantly the hill was covered with the little people, dancing and tossing their caps about. One of these fell near John: he caught it, and set it on his head. By the acquisition of this cap he had obtained power over the elves. When the cock began to crow, a bright glass point appeared on the hill-top, and opened. John and the people descended, and he found himself in a land of wonder. He found that there were in that place the most beautiful walks, in which he might ramble along for miles in all directions without ever finding an end of them, so immensely large was the hill that the little people lived in; and yet outwardly it seemed but a little hill, with a few bushes and trees growing on it. It was extraordinary that, between the meads and fields, which were thick sown with hills and lakes and islands, and ornamented with trees and flowers in the greatest variety, there ran, as it were, small lanes, through which, as through crystal rocks, one was obliged to pass to come to any new place; and the single meads and fields were often a mile long, and the flowers were so brilliant and so fragrant, and the song of the numerous birds so sweet, that John had never seen any thing on earth at all like it. There was a breeze, and yet one did not feel the wind; it was quite clear and bright, and yet there was no heat, no sun, no moon; the waves dashed about, but there was no danger; and the most beautiful little barks and canoes came, like white swans, when one wanted to cross the water, and went back-wards and forwards of themselves. Whence all this came no one knew, nor could his servant tell any thing about it; but one thing John saw plainly, which was, that the large carbuncles and diamonds that were set in the roof and walls gave light instead of the sun, moon, and stars. Here John found a little maiden, Elizabeth Krabbin, daughter of the minister of Rambin, who had been spirited away by the little people a few years before. John and she soon formed an attachment, and were wont to walk together. On one of their strolls they must have approached the surface, for they heard the crowing of a cock. At the sound, the remembrance of earth returned to them, and they felt a desire once more to be on Christian land. 'Everything down here,' said Elizabeth, 'is beautiful, and the little folk are kind, but there is not pure pleasure here. Every night I dream of my father and mother, and of our churchyard; and I cannot go to the House of God, and worship Him as a Christian should; for this is no Christian life we lead down here, but a delusive, half-heathen one.'

John, however, could not release Elizabeth from the power of the underground folk till he found a toad, the sight and smell of which was so repulsive to them, that they readily compiled with every request of John, on condition he should bury the offensive reptile.

Then he and the girl escaped, taking with them gold and silver and jewels, to such an amount, that their fortune was made. They were, of course, married; and John bought up half the island of Rügen, was ennobled, built and endowed the present church of Rambin, and became the founder of a powerful family. To the altar of Rambin he gave some of the cups and plates of gold made by the underground people, and his own and Elizabeth's glass shoes which they had worn in the mount. But these were taken away in the time of Charles XII of Sweden, when the Russians came on the island, and the Cossacks plundered the churches.

In the year 1520, there lived at Basle, in Switzerland, a tailor's son, named Leonard. He entered a cave which penetrated far into the bowels of the earth, holding a consecrated taper in his hand. He came to an enchanted land, where was a beautiful woman wearing a golden crown, but from her waist downwards she was a serpent. She gave him gold and silver, and entreated him to kiss her three times. He complied twice, but the writhing of her tail so horrified him, that he fled without giving her the third kiss. Afterwards he prowled about the mountains, seeking the entrance to the cave, filled with a craving for the society of the lady, but he never could find it again.

There is a curious story told by Fordun in his 'Scotichronicon', by Matthew of Westminster in his Chronicle, and by Roger of Wendover in his 'Flowers of History', which has some interest in connexion with the legend of the Tanhäuser. They relate that in the year 1050, a youth of noble birth had been married in Rome, and during the nuptial feast, being engaged in a game of ball, he took off his wedding-ring, and placed it on the finger of a statue of Venus. When he wished to resume it, he found that the stony hand had become clenched, so that it was impossible to remove the ring. Thenceforth he was haunted by the Goddess Venus, who constantly whispered in his ear, 'Embrace me; I am Venus, whom you have wedded; I will never restore your ring.' However, by the assistance of a priest, she was at length forced to give it up to its rightful owner.

This story occurs also in Vincent of Beauvais. . . . Cæsarius of Heisterbach has also a story bearing a relation to that of Venus and the ring. A certain Clerk Phillip, a great necromancer, took some Swabian and Bavarian youths to a lonely spot in a field, where, at their desire, he proceeded to perform incantations. First he drew a circle round them with his sword, and warned them on no consideration to leave the ring. Then retiring from them a little space he began his incantations, and suddenly there appeared around the youths a multitude of armed men, brandishing weapons, and daring them to fight. The demons, failing to draw them by this means from their enchanted circle, vanished, and then there was seen a company of beautiful damsels, dancing about the ring, and by their attitudes alluring the youths towards them. One of these, exceeding the others in beauty and grace, singled out a youth, and dancing before him, extended to him a ring of gold, casting languishing glances towards him, and by all means in her power endeavouring to attract his attention, and kindle his passion. The young man, unable any longer to resist, put forth his finger beyond the circle to the ring, and the apparition at once drew him towards her and vanished along with him. However, after much trouble, the necromancer was able to recover him from the embraces of the evil spirit.

Another mediæval story is founded on the same myth, but purified and Christianized. A knight is playing at ball, and incommoded by his ring. He therefore removes it, and places it for safety on the finger of a statue of the Blessed Virgin Mary. On seeking it again he finds the hand of the figure clasped, and he is unable to recover his ring. Whereupon the knight renounces the world, and as the betrothed of the Virgin enters a monastery.

The incident of the ring in connexion with the ancient goddess is certainly taken from the old religion of the Teutonic and Scandinavian peoples. Freyja was represented in her temples holding a ring in her hand; so was Thorgerda Hörgabrúda. The Faereyinga Saga relates an event in the life of the Faroese hero, Sigmund Brestesson, which is to the point. 'They (Earl Hakon and Sigmund) went to the temple, and the earl fell on the ground before her statue, and there he lay long. The statue was richly dressed, and had a heavy gold ring on the arm. And the earl stood up and touched the ring, and tried to remove it, but could not; and it seemed to Sigmund as though she frowned. Then the earl said, "She is not pleased with thee, Sigmund! and I do not know whether I shall be able to reconcile you; but that shall be the token of her favour, if she gives us the ring, which she has in her hand." Then the earl took much silver, and laid it on the footstool before her; and again he flung himself prostrate before her, and Sigmund noticed that he wept profusely. And when he stood up he took the ring, and she let go of it. Then the earl gave it to Sigmund, and said, "I give thee this ring to thy weal, never part with it." And Sigmund promised he would not.' This ring is the death of the Faroese chief. In after years, King Olaf, who converts him to Christianity, knowing that this gold ring is a relic of Paganism, asks Sigmund to give it him. The chief refuses, and the king angrily pronounces a warning that it will be the cause of his death. And his word falls true, for Sigmund is murdered in his sleep for the sake of the ring.

Unquestionably the Venus of the Hörselberg, of Basle, of the Eildon Hill, that of whom Fordun, Vincent, and Cæsarius relate such weird tales, is the ancient goddess Holda, or Thorgerda; a conclusion to which the stories of the ring naturally lead us.

The classic legend of Ulysses held captive for eight years by the nymph Calypso in the island of Ogygia, and again for one year by the enchantress Circe, contains the root of the same story of the Tanhäuser.

What may have been the significance of the primeval story-radical it is impossible for us now to ascertain; but the legend, as it shaped itself in the Middle Ages, is certainly indicative of the struggle between the new and the old faith.

We see thinly veiled in Tanhäuser, the story of a man, Christian in name, but heathen at heart, allured by the attractions of Paganism, which seems to satisfy his poetic instincts, and which gives full rein to his passions. But these excesses pall on him after a while, and the religion of sensuality leaves a great void in his breast.

He turns to Christianity, and at first it seems to promise all that he requires. But alas! he is repelled by its ministers. On all sides he is met by practice widely at variance with profession. Pride, worldliness, want of sympathy, exist among those who should be the foremost to guide, sustain, and receive him. All the warm springs which gushed up in his broken heart are choked, his softened spirit is hardened again, and he returns in despair to bury his sorrows, and drown his anxieties, in the debauchery of his former creed.

A sad picture, but doubtless one very true.

CHAPTER 7

The Terrestrial Paradise

HE SUBJECT of this chapter reflects back to the first, in which we saw how the semi-mythical kingdom of Prester John reflected, and was based upon, the ideas of an earthly paradise. It is also a natural outcropping of the previous chapter, in which we saw that the journey to Venusberg was influenced by visions of the Otherworld from many different cultures. Both themes reflect the human desire to reach a paradisal state of being, and the belief that, in some way, Paradise could, and did, exist in the physical realm of Earth. Naturally, in the descriptions which have come down to us, from biblical texts to the medieval chronicles quoted below, everything is bigger, finer, more beautiful and richer than anything to which we have access in the outside world. It is like the accompanying myth of the Golden Age, a time and place to which we might all with good reason aspire to go.

However, Paradise remains significantly beyond reach, protected either by angels with fiery swords, walls of flame, or rivers which cannot be crossed. There is no escaping the fact that, in the West at least, we have perceived ourselves for a long time as exiles from Eden – cast out of the paradise on earth which was once our home. It can be argued that the whole of the Western cultural approach to the world in which we live and have our being grows out of this belief – to the extent that we have never ceased trying to recreate an earthly paradise whatever the cost to ourselves, our neighbours and the earth on which we walk.

This idea is one that has emerged again and again in the spirituality and literatures of both East and West. It is present in Buddhist teaching, in Islamic belief, in Native American spirituality, and it is to be found (randomly) in the myths of classical Greece, in the voyage of the Argonauts to find the Golden Fleece, in Diodorus Siculus's account of the Hyperboreans who lived 'behind the North Wind', in Dante's *Divine Comedy* and in the writings of John Milton, Plato's *Republic*, Thomas More's *Utopia*, and the prophetic writings of William Blake. In modern times it is expressed by such successful novels as James Hilton's *Lost Horizon* (1927) or in the writings of Frank Herbert (*Dune*), in Doris Lessing's Shikasta (1981–9) series and Ursula le Guin's *Earthsea* books. It is implicit in many episodes of the phenomenally successful TV series *Star Trek*, which reflects the humanistic vision of its creator, Gene Roddenberry. All, in their own way, reflect a desire which is still as current today as it ever was – a desire to find a way, while still in the body, to a perfect realm where all is well, where there is neither 'frost nor snow, hail nor rain; but there is . . . the well of life'.

Gould is wrong in his assumptions regarding the Celtic voyages to the Otherworld, of which he mentions only one, that of St Brendan (or Brandon). This was certainly not 'founded on that of Sinbad', but is part of an established tradition of Voyage texts known collectively as 'Immrama'. The best of these is 'The Voyage of Maelduin' (*c*.950) which describes the journey of the hero to a number of islands, each one peopled by more and more fantastic beings. This has been shown to be an allegorical account of the soul's journey and, as such, most of the Immrama are to be read. They can offer profound spiritual insights, and portray the hunger of the human soul for Paradise.

Neither would I agree that these texts are in any way related to what Gould refers to as 'the paradise of Druid Mythology – an idea based on the misunderstanding of late "revivalist" texts of Druidry'. The true Celtic traditions abound in descriptions of the Otherworld, many of which bear a striking resemblance to the later versions of the medieval writers quoted below. The following example, describing the Plain of Honey or Mag Mell, is from the Middle Irish text known as *The Sickbed of Cuchullain*:

> There is a tree at the door of the court
> It cannot be matched in harmony,
> A tree of silver upon which the sun shines,
> Like unto gold is its splendid lustre.
>
> There at the eastern door
> Three stately trees of crimson hue,
> From which the birds of perpetual bloom
> Sing to the youth from the kingly fort.

Such descriptions cannot fail to evoke a response in all of us. Even the word Paradise comes from the Persian and means a garden or pleasure park. We long to walk there, to breathe the scents of the myriad flowers, and to meet the divine and wondrous beings whose habitation it is.

*　　*　　*

THE exact position of Eden, and its present condition, does not seem to have occupied the minds of our Anglo-Saxon ancestors, nor to have given rise among them to wild speculations.

The map of the tenth century in the British Museum, accompanying the Periegesis of Priscian, is far more correct than the generality of maps which we find in MSS at a later period; and Paradise does not occupy the place of Cochin China, or the isles of Japan, as it did later, after that the fabulous voyage of S. Brandan had become popular in the eleventh century. The site, however, had been already indicated by Cosmas, who wrote in the seventh century, and had been specified by him as occupying a continent east of China, beyond the ocean, and still watered by the four great rivers Pison, Gihon, Hiddekel, and Euphrates, which sprang from subterranean canals. In a map of the ninth century, preserved in the Strasbourg Library, the terrestrial Paradise is, however, on the Continent, placed at the extreme east of Asia; in fact, is situated in the Celestial Empire. It occupies the same position in a Turin MS, and also in a map accompanying a commentary on the Apocalypse in the British Museum.

According to the fictitious letter of Prester John to the Emperor Emanuel Comnenus, Paradise was situated close to – within three days' journey of – his own territories, but where those territories were, is not distinctly specified.

'The river Indus, which issues out of Paradise,' writes the mythical king, 'flows among the plains, through a certain province, and it expands, embracing the whole province with its various windings: there are found emeralds, sapphires, carbuncles, topazes, chrysolites, onyx, beryl, sardius, and many other precious stones. There too grows the plant called Asbestos.' A wonderful fountain, moreover, breaks out at the roots of Olympus, a mountain in Prester John's domain, and 'from hour to hour, and day by day, the taste of this fountain varies; and its source is hardly three days' journey from Paradise, from which Adam was expelled. If any man drinks thrice of this spring, he will from that day feel no infirmity, and he will, as long as he lives, appear of the age of thirty.' This Olympus is a corruption of Alumbo, which is no other than Columbo in Ceylon, as is abundantly evident from Sir John Mandeville's Travels, though this important fountain has escaped the observation of Sir Emmerson Tennant.

'Toward the heed of that forest (he writes) is the cytee of Polombe, and above the city is a great mountayne, also clept Polombe. And of that mount, the Cytee hathe his name. And at the foot of that Mount is a fayr welle and a gret that hathe odour and savour of all spices; and at every hour of the day, he chaungethe his odour and his savour dyversely. And whoso drynkethe 3 times fasting of that watre of that welle, he is hool of alle maner sykenesse, that he hathe. And thei that duellen there and drynken often of that welle, thei nevere han sykenesse, and thei semen alle weys yonge. I have dronken there of 3 or 4 sithes; and zit, methinkethe, I fare the better. Some men clepen it the Welle of Youthe: for thei that often drynken thereat, semen alle weys yongly, and lyven withouten sykenesse. And men seyn, that that welle comethe out of Paradys: and therefore it is so vertuous.'

Gautier de Metz, in his poem on the 'Image du Monde', written in the thirteenth century, places the terrestrial Paradise in an unapproachable region of Asia, surrounded by flames, and having an armed angel to guard the only gate.

Lambertus Floridus, in a MS of the twelfth century, preserved in the Imperial Library in Paris, describes it as 'Paradisus insula in oceano in oriente': and in the map accompanying it, Paradise is represented as an island, a little south-east of Asia, surrounded by rays, and at some distance from the mainland; and in another MS of the same library – a mediæval encyclopædia – under the word Paradisus is a passage which states that in the centre of Paradise is a fountain which waters the garden – that in fact described by Prester John, and that of which story-telling Sir John Mandeville declared he had 'dronken 3 or 4 sithes'. Close to this fountain is the Tree of Life. The temperature of the country is equable; neither frosts nor burning heats destroy the vegetation. The four rivers already mentioned rise in it. Paradise is, however, inaccessible to the traveller, on account of the wall of fire which surrounds it.

Paludanus relates in his 'Thesaurus Novus', of course on incontrovertible authority, that Alexander the Great was full of desire to see the terrestrial Paradise, and that he undertook his wars in the East for the express purpose of reaching it, and obtaining admission into it. He states that on his nearing Eden an old man was captured in a ravine by some of Alexander's soldiers, and they were about to conduct him to their monarch, when the venerable man said, 'Go and announce to Alexander that it is in vain he seeks Paradise; his efforts will be perfectly fruitless, for the way of Paradise is the way of humility, a way of which he knows nothing. Take this stone and give it to Alexander, and say to him, "From this stone learn what you must think of yourself."' Now this stone was of great value and excessively heavy, outweighing and excelling in value all other gems, but when reduced to powder it was as light as a tuft of hay, and as worthless. By which token the mysterious old man meant, that Alexander alive was the greatest of monarchs, but Alexander dead would be a thing of nought.

That strangest of mediæval preachers, Meffreth, who got into trouble by denying the Immaculate Conception of the Blessed Virgin, in his second sermon for the Third Sunday in Advent, discusses the locality of the terrestrial Paradise, and claims S. Basil and S. Ambrose as his authorities for stating that it is situated on the top of a very lofty mountain in Eastern Asia; so lofty indeed is the mountain, that the waters of the four rivers fall in cascade down to a lake at its foot, with such a roar that the natives who live on the shores of the lake are stone-deaf. Meffreth also explains the escape of Paradise from submergence at the Deluge, on the same grounds as does the Master of Sentences, by the mountain being so very high that the waters which rose over Ararat were only able to wash its base.

A manuscript in the British Museum tells us that 'Paradise is neither in heaven nor on earth. The book says that Noah's flood was forty fathoms high, over the highest hills that are on earth; and Paradise is forty fathoms higher than Noah's flood was, and it hangeth between heaven and earth wonderfully, as the ruler of all things made it. And it is perfectly level both in length and breadth. There is neither hollow nor hill; nor is there frost nor snow, hail nor rain; but there is fons vitæ, that is the well of life. When the calends of January commence, then floweth the well so beautifully and so gently, and no deeper than man may wet his finger on the front, over all that land. And so likewise each month, once when the month comes in the well begins to flow. And there is the copse of wood, which is called Radion Saltus, where each tree is as straight as an arrow, and so high, that no earthly man ever saw so high, or can say of what kind they are. And there never falleth leaf off, for they are ever-green, beautiful, and pleasant, full of happiness. Paradise is upright on the eastern part of this world. There is neither heat nor hunger, nor is there ever night, but always day. The sun there shineth seven times brighter than on this earth. Therein dwell innumerable angels of God with the holy souls till doomsday. Therein dwelleth

71

a beautiful bird called Phœnix; he is large and grand, as the Mighty One formed him; he is the lord over all birds.'

The monk who incited S. Brandan to undertake his mythical voyage told him that he had sailed due east from Ireland, and had come at last to Paradise, which was an island full of joy and mirth, and the earth as bright as the sun, and it was a glorious sight; and the half-year he was there slipped by as a few moments. On his return to the abbey, his garments were still fragrant with the odours of Paradise. Brandan also arrived at the same island, and with his companions traversed it for the space of forty days without meeting any one, till he came to a broad river, on the banks of which stood a young man, who told him that this stream divided the world in twain; and that none living might cross it.

In a MS volume in the library of Corpus Christi College, Cambridge, is a map of the world, dating from the twelfth century, whereon Paradise is figured as an island opposite the mouth of the Ganges, which flows into the ocean somewhere about where the Amour in reality empties itself.

The Anglo-Saxon poem, 'De Phœnice', in the Exeter book, a translation of the work of the Pseudo-Lactantius, asserts:–

> I have heard tell
> That there is far hence
> In eastern parts
> A land most noble,
> Amongst men renowned.
> That tract of earth is not
> Over mid earth
> Fellow to many
> Peopled lands;
> But it is withdrawn
> Through the Creator's might
> From wicked doers.
> Beauteous is all the plain,
> With delights blessed,
> With the sweetest
> Of earth's odours.

And then it rambles on in description of its delights, which may be imagined without further quotation.

The Hereford map of the thirteenth century represents the terrestrial Paradise as a circular island near India, cut off from the continent not only by the sea, but also by a battlemented wall, with a gateway to the west.

Rupert of Duytz regards it as having been situated in Armenia. Radulphus Highden, in the thirteenth century, relying on the authority of S. Basil and S. Isidore of Seville, places Eden in an inaccessible region of Oriental Asia; and this was also the opinion of Philostorgus. Hugo de S. Victor, in his book 'De Situ Terrarum', expresses himself thus:– 'Paradise is a spot in the Orient productive of all kinds of woods and pomiferous trees. It contains the Tree of Life: there is neither cold nor heat there, but perpetual equable temperature. It contains a fountain which flows forth in four rivers.'

Rabanus Maurus, with more discretion, says:– 'Many folk want to make out that the site of Paradise is in the east of the earth, though cut off by the longest intervening space of ocean or earth from all regions which man now inhabits. Consequently, the waters of the Deluge, which covered the highest points of the surface of our orb, were unable to reach it. However, whether it be there, or whether it be any where else, God knows; but that there *was* such a spot once, and that it was on earth, that is certain.'

Jacques de Vitry ('Historia Orientalis'), Gervais of Tilbury, in his 'Otia Imperalia', and many others, hold the same views as to the site of Paradise that were entertained by Hugo de S. Victor.

Jourdain de Sèverac, monk and traveller in the beginning of the fourteenth century, places the terrestrial Paradise in the 'Third India'; that is to say, in trans-Gangic India.

Leonardo Dati, a Florentine poet of the fifteenth century, composed a geographical treatise in verse, entitled 'Della Sfera'; and it is in Asia that he locates the garden:–

> Asia è le prima parte dove l'huomo
> Sendo innocente stava in Paradiso.

But perhaps the most remarkable account of the terrestrial Paradise ever furnished, is that of the 'Eireks Saga Vídförla', an Icelandic narrative of the fourteenth century, giving the adventures of a certain Norwegian, named Eirek, who had vowed, whilst a heathen, that he would explore the fabulous Deathless Land of pagan Scandinavian mythology. The romance is possibly a Christian recension of an ancient heathen myth; and Paradise has taken the place in it of Glœsisvellir.

According to the majority of the MSS the story purports to be nothing more than a religious novel; but one audacious copyist has ventured to assert that it is all fact, and that the details are taken down from the lips of those who heard them from Eirek himself. The account is briefly this:–

Eirek was a son of Thrand, king of Drontheim, and having taken upon him a vow to explore the Deathless Land, he went to Denmark, where he picked up a friend of the same name as himself. They then went to Constantinople, and called upon the Emperor, who held a long conversation with them, which is duly reported, relative to the truths of Christianity and the site of the Deathless Land, which, he assures them, is nothing more nor less than Paradise.

'The world,' said the monarch, who had not forgotten his geography since he left school, 'is precisely 180,000 stages round (about 1,000,000 English miles), and it is not propped up on posts – not a bit! – it is supported by the power of God; and the distance between earth and heaven is 100,045 miles (another MS reads 9382 miles – the difference is immaterial); and round about the earth is a big sea called Ocean.' 'And what's to the south of the earth?' asked Eirek. 'Oh! there is the end of the world, and that is India.' 'And pray where am I to find the Deathless Land?' 'Paradise, I suppose you mean – lies slightly east of India.'

Having obtained this information, the two Eireks started, furnished with letters from the Greek Emperor.

They traversed Syria, and took ship – probably at Balsora; then, reaching India, they proceeded on their journey on horseback, till they came to a dense forest, the gloom of which was so great, through the interlacing of the boughs, that even by day the stars could be observed twinkling, as though they were seen from the bottom of a well.

On emerging from the forest, the two Eireks came upon a strait, separating them from a beautiful land, which was unmistakably Paradise; and the Danish Eirek, intent on displaying his Scriptural knowledge, pronounced the strait to be the river Pison. This was crossed by a stone bridge, guarded by a dragon.

The Danish Eirek, deterred by the prospect of an encounter with this monster, refused to advance, and even endeavoured to persuade his friend to give up the attempt to enter Paradise as hopeless, after that they had come within sight of the favoured land. But the Norseman deliberately walked, sword in hand, into the maw of the dragon, and next moment, to his infinite surprise and delight, found himself liberated from the gloom of the monster's interior, and safely placed in Paradise.

'The land was most beautiful, and the grass as gorgeous as purple; it was studded with flowers, and was traversed by honey rills. The land was extensive and level, so that there was not to be seen mountain or hill, and the sun shone cloudless without night and darkness; the calm of the air was great, and there was but a feeble murmur of wind, and that which there was, breathed redolent with the odour of blossoms.' After a short walk, Eirek observed what certainly must have been a remarkable object, namely, a tower or steeple self-suspended in the air, without any support whatever, though access might be had to it by means of a slender ladder. By this Eirek ascended into a loft of the tower, and found there an excellent cold collation prepared for him. After having partaken of this he went to sleep, and in vision beheld and conversed with his guardian angel, who promised to conduct him back to his father-land, but to come for him again, and fetch him away from it for ever at the expiration of the tenth year after his return to Drontheim.

Eirek then retraced his steps to India, unmolested by the dragon, which did not affect any surprise at having to disgorge him, and, indeed, which seems to have been, notwithstanding his looks, but a harmless and passive dragon.

After a tedious journey of seven years, Eirek teached his native land, where he related his adventures, to the confusion of the heathen, and to the delight and edification of the faithful. 'And in the tenth year, and at break of day, as Eirek went to prayer, God's Spirit caught him away, and he was never seen again in this world: so here ends all we have to say of him.'

The Saga, of which I have given the merest outline, is certainly striking, and contains some beautiful passages. It follows the commonly-received opinion which identified Paradise with Ceylon; and, indeed, an earlier Icelandic work, the 'Rym begla', indicates the locality of the terrestrial Paradise as being near India, for it speaks of the Ganges as taking its rise in the mountains of Eden. It is not unlikely that the curious history of Eirek, is a translation, with modifications, of a Keltic romance. I form this opinion from the introduction of the bridge over which Eirek has to pass, and the marvellous house suspended in air, which is an item peculiar to the Paradise of Druidical Mythology.

Later than the fifteenth century, we find no theories propounded concerning the terrestrial Paradise, though there are many treaties on the presumed situation of the ancient Eden. At Madrid was published a poem on the subject, entitled 'Patriana decas', in 1629. In 1662 G. C. Kirchmayer, a Wittemberg professor, composed a thoughtful dissertation, 'De Paradiso', which he inserted in his 'Deliciæ Æstivæ'. Fr. Arnoulx wrote a work on Paradise in 1665, full of the grossest absurdities. In 1666 appeared Carver's 'Discourse on the Terrestrian Paradise'. Bochart composed a tract on the subject; Huet wrote on it also, and his work passed through seven editions, the last dated from Amsterdam, 1701. The Père Hardouin composed a 'Nouveau Traité de la Situation du Paradis Terrestre', La Haye, 1730. An Armenian work on the rivers of Paradise was translated by M. Saint Martin in 1819; and in 1842 Sir W. Ouseley read a paper on the situation of Eden, before the Literary Society in London.

CHAPTER 8

Melusine

HE STORY of Melusine (or Melusina as Gould prefers to call her) is one which is told, in various forms, in many different parts of the world. It reflects a deeper theme, on which we have already touched in 'The Mountain of Venus' – the desire of human men for faery wives (it is less often that women seek faery men or, indeed, contract marriages with them) and that of the people of Faery for human consorts. It has been suggested that one of the reasons for this 'inter-species' mating is the need of the faery race for human genes, and that those of pure faery blood cannot bear children (hence the stories of changelings, strange non-human offspring left in place of stolen human children). One does not need to look so far to find the cause of the human fascination with faery women – the race is remarkable for its beauty and in all of such stories the women met with at fountains or by rivers or at sea are without exception glorious.

In the case of the Mermaid, who is half fish and half woman, this seems to be a deeper representation of the double nature of these Otherworldly beings, who are neither wholly human nor wholly of Faery but who partake of both natures.

The story of Melusine herself appears to have grown out of a whole clutch of circumstances. Undoubtedly it must have been circulating, in one form or another, for many hundreds of years before it became centred on the House of Anjou. It was probably first told of Count Fulke Nerra (the black) who was supposed to have lived a life of such surpassing wickedness that it was hardly surprising if he ended up married to a woman who was half serpent and therefore undoubtedly an offspring of the Devil. The same story (or a variant of it) was told of another Fulke – le Rechin, the quarrelsome – who has a number of wives; he would simply send one away before introducing another into his life. Of this character the following variant of the story is told.

76

Count Fulke ruled in the country of Angiers, and one day he returned home with a beautiful new wife, who soon bore him four children and who was well liked by the people in the Count's domain. In every way she seemed ordinary except one – she seldom attended Mass in the church, and always seemed to find a reason for leaving before the consecration of the sacraments. Eventually Faulk became aware of this curious behaviour and called upon four of his knights to help discover the reason for it. He asked them to contrive to stand upon the long train of his wife's cloak, thus preventing her usual rapid exit. Shortly before the time came for the consecration, the lady appeared to recollect something she had forgotten and made to leave. The knights stood upon her cloak and as the Host was raised she gave a shriek and flew out of the window, carrying two of the children with her. From the two who survived, the family of the Counts of Anjou, including Raymond of Poitiers, were descended – hence the widespread belief that this powerful family was descended from the Devil!

The version recalled by Gould reflects an earlier arc of the story which was not recorded in written form until much later. Jean d'Arras seems to have been responsible for some of the more colourful aspects of the story, including the strange deformed children to which the lady gave birth – a factor which might well have suggested that something was amiss, both to the Count and to his courtiers.

The story has continued to flourish through the traditions which tell of the appearance of Melusine and the cry she gives forth whenever danger threatens one of the Lusignan family, or when a new Count is about to be born. This last attribute, as mentioned by Gould, relates her to the Irish Banshee, who behaves in a similar fashion when death threatens certain families. This confirms her identity as a faery being, since Banshee is a corruption of *Bean Sidhe* or Woman of the Sidhe, the faery race of the Celts.

The appearance of Melusine and her sisters beside a fountain further confirms this, since in nearly every instance of the many stories which refer to faery women the setting is of this kind; indeed, the links with water run through a high preponderance of the stories of faery women – a fact which Gould rightly ascribes to a Celtic source.

One of the best-known Celtic instances of the story from which the Melusine myth developed is that of the Lady of Llyn Y Fan Fach, a mountain lake near Llanddeusant in Wales. In this tale a farmer of Myddfai fell in love with a beautiful woman he met beside the lake. She promised to marry him and bear him children as long as he never struck her. To this he agreed, but eventually, as is ever the case in these stories, he forgot his promise, at which the Lady, like Melusine, went back into the lake. She reappeared thereafter from time to time, and taught her children medicine. They became a famous family of healers, and to this day many of their recipes for herbal remedies are made and sold by their descendants.

Likewise the story of Melusine has continued to excite interest and to be remembered in the folk tradition of France. Ginger cakes called Melusines, baked in the form of a woman with a serpent's tail, are still sold at the May Day fair in Poitiers, and in 1983 a wonderful novelization of the story appeared, incorporating every scrap of lore concerning Melusine, from the pen of Manuel Mujica Lainez.

*   *   *

EMMERICK, Count of Poitou, was a nobleman of great wealth, and eminent for his virtues. He had two children, a son named Bertram, and a daughter Blaniferte. In the great forest which stretched away in all directions around the knoll on which stood the town and castle of Poictiers, lived a Count de la Forêt, related to Emmerick, but poor and with a large family. Out of compassion for his kinsman, the Count of Poitou adopted his youngest son Raymond, a beautiful and amiable youth, and made him his constant companion in hall and in the chase. One day the Count and his retinue hunted a boar in the forest of Colombiers, and distancing his servants, Emmerick found himself alone in the depths of the wood with Raymond. The boar had escaped. Night came on, and the two huntsmen lost their way. They succeeded in lighting a fire, and were warming themselves over the blaze, when suddenly the boar plunged out of the forest upon the Count, and Raymond, snatching up his sword, struck at the beast, but the blade glanced off and slew the Count. A second blow laid the boar at his side. Raymond then with horror perceived that his friend and master was dead. In despair he mounted his horse and fled, not knowing whither he went.

Presently the boughs of the trees became less interlaced, and the trunks fewer; next moment his horse, crashing through the shrubs, brought him out on a pleasant glade, white with rime, and illumined by the new moon; in the midst bubbled up a limpid fountain, and flowed away over a pebbly floor with a soothing murmur. Near the fountainhead sat three maidens in glimmering white dresses, with long waving golden hair, and faces of inexpressible beauty.

Raymond was riveted to the spot with astonishment. He believed that he saw a vision of angels, and would have prostrated himself at their feet, had not one of them advanced and stayed him. The lady inquired the cause of his manifest terror, and the young man, after a slight hesitation, told her of his dreadful misfortune. She listened with attention, and at the conclusion of his story, recommended him to remount his horse, and gallop out of the forest, and return to Poictiers, as though unconscious of what had taken place. All the huntsmen had that day lost themselves in the wood, and were returning singly, at intervals, to the castle, so that no suspicion would attach to him. The body of the Count would be found, and from the proximity of the dead boar, it would be concluded that he had fallen before the tusk of the animal, to which he had given its death-blow.

Relieved of his anxiety, Raymond was able to devote his attention exclusively to the beauty of the lady who addressed him, and found means to prolong the conversation till daybreak. He had never beheld charms equal to hers, and the susceptible heart of the youth was completely captivated by the fair unknown. Before he left her, he obtained from her a promise to be his. She then told him to ask of his kinsman. Bertram, as a gift, so much ground around the fountain where they had met, as could be covered by a stag's hide: upon this ground she undertook to erect a magnificent palace. Her name, she told him, was Melusina; she was a water-fay of great power and wealth. His she consented to be, but subject to one condition, that her Saturdays might be spent in a complete seclusion, upon which he should never venture to intrude.

Raymond then left her, and followed her advice to the letter. Bertram, who succeeded his father, readily granted the land he asked for, but was not a little vexed, when he found that, by cutting the hide into threads, Raymond had succeeded in making it include a considerable area.

Raymond then invited the young Count to his wedding, and the marriage festivities took place, with unusual splendour, in the magnificent castle erected by Melusina. On the evening of the marriage, the bride, with tears in her beautiful eyes, implored her husband on no account to attempt an intrusion on her privacy upon Saturdays, for such an intrusion must infallibly separate them for ever. The enamoured Raymond readily swore to strictly observe her wishes in this matter.

Melusina continued to extend the castle, and strengthen its fortifications, till the like was not to be seen in all the country round. On its completion she named it after herself Lusinia, a name which has been corrupted into Lusignan, which it bears to this day.

In course of time, the Lady of Lusignan gave birth to a son, who was baptized Urian. He was a strangely shaped child: his mouth was large, his ears pendulous; one of his eyes was red, the other green.

A twelvemonth later she gave birth to another son, whom she called Gedes; he had a face which was scarlet. In thank-offering for his birth she erected and endowed the convent of Malliers; and, as a place of residence for her child, built the strong castle of Favent.

Melusina then bore a third son, who was christened Gyot. He was a fine, handsome child, but one of his eyes was higher up in his face than the other. For him his mother built La Rochelle.

Her next son, Anthony, had long claws on his fingers, and was covered with hair; the next again had but a single eye. The sixth was Geoffry with the Tooth, so called from a boar's tusk which protruded from his jaw. Other children she had, but all were in some way disfigured and monstrous.

Years passed, and the love of Raymond for his beautiful wife never languished. Every Saturday she left him, and spent the twenty-four hours in the strictest seclusion, without her husband thinking of intruding on her privacy. The children grew up to be great heroes and illustrious warriors. One, Freimund, entered the Church, and became a pious monk, in the abbey of Malliers. The aged Count de la Forêt and the brothers of Raymond shared in his good fortune, and the old man spent his last years in the castle with his son, whilst the brothers were furnished with money and servants suitable to their rank.

One Saturday, the old father inquired at dinner after his daughter-in-law. Raymond replied that she was not visible on Saturdays. Thereupon one of his brothers, drawing him aside, whispered that strange gossiping tales were about relative to this sabbath seclusion, and that it behoved him to inquire into it, and set the minds of people at rest. Full of wrath and anxiety, the Count rushed off to the private apartments of the Countess, but found them empty. One door alone was locked, and that opened into a bath. He looked through the keyhole, and to his dismay beheld her in the water, her lower extremities changed into the tail of a monstrous fish or serpent.

Silently he withdrew. No word of what he had seen passed his lips; it was not

loathing that filled his heart, but anguish at the thought that by his fault he must lose the beautiful wife who had been the charm and glory of his life. Some time passed by, however, and Melusina gave no token of consciousness that she had been observed during the period of her transformation. But one day news reached the castle that Geoffry with the Tooth had attacked the monastery of Malliers, and burned it; and that in the flames had perished Freimund, with the abbot and a hundred monks. On hearing of this disaster, the poor father, in a paroxysm of misery, exclaimed, as Melusina approached to comfort him, 'Away, odious serpent, contaminator of my honourable race!'

At these words she fainted; and Raymond, full of sorrow for having spoken thus intemperately, strove to revive her. When she came to herself again, with streaming tears she kissed and embraced him for the last time. 'O husband!' she said, 'I leave two little ones in their cradle; look tenderly after them, bereaved of their mother. And now farewell for ever! yet know that thou, and those who succeed thee, shall see me hover over this fair castle of Lusignan, whenever a new lord is to come.' And with a long wail of agony she swept from the window, leaving the impression of her foot on the stone she last touched.

The children in arms she had left were Dietrich and Raymond. At night, the nurses beheld a glimmering figure appear near the cradle of the babes, most like the vanished Countess, but from her waist downwards terminating in a scaly fish-tail enamelled blue and white. At her approach the little ones extended their arms and smiled, and she took them to her breast and suckled them; but as the grey dawn stole in at the casement, she vanished, and the children's cries told the nurses that their mother was gone.

Long was it believed in France that the unfortunate Melusina appeared in the air, wailing over the ramparts of Lusignan before the death of one of its lords; and that, on the extinction of the family, she was seen whenever a king of France was to depart this life. Mézeray informs us that he was assured of the truth of the appearance of Melusina on the old tower of Lusignan, previous to the death of one of her descendants, or of a king of France, by people of reputation, and who were not by any means credulous. She appeared in a mourning dress, and continued for a long time to utter the most heart-rending lamentations.

Brantôme, in his eulogium on the Duke of Montpensier, who in 1574 destroyed Lusignan, a Huguenot retreat, says:

'I heard, more than forty years ago, an old veteran say, that when the Emperor Charles V came to France, they brought him by Lusignan for the sake of the recreation of hunting the deer, which were then in great abundance in the fine old parks of France; that he was never tired of admiring and praising the beauty, the size, and the chef d'œuvre of that house, built, which is more, by such a lady, of whom he made them tell him several fabulous tales, which are there quite common, even to the good old women who washed their linen at the fountains, whom Queen Catherine de Medicis, mother of the king, would also question and listen to. Some told her that they used sometimes to see her come to the fountain, to bathe in it, in the form of a most beautiful woman and in the dress of a widow. Others said that they used to see her, but very rarely, and that on Saturday evening (for in that state she did not let herself be seen), bathing, half her body being that of a very beautiful lady, the other half ending in a snake; others, that she used to appear a-top of the great tower in a very beautiful form, and as a snake. Some said, that when any great disaster was to come on the kingdom, or a change of reign, or a death, or misfortune among her relatives, who were the greatest people of France, and were kings, that three days before she was heard to cry, with a cry most shrill and terrible, three times.

'This is held to be perfectly true. Several persons of that place, who have heard it, are positive of it, and hand it from father to son; and say that, even when the siege came on, many soldiers and men of honour, who were there, affirmed it. But it was when order was given to throw down and destroy her castles, that she uttered her loudest cries and wails. Since then she has not been heard. Some old wives, however, say she has appeared to them, but very rarely.'

In 1387, Jean d'Arras, secretary to the Duke of Berry, received orders from his master to collect all information attainable with reference to Melusina, probably for the entertainment of the sister of the duke, the Countess de Bar. This he did, making considerable use of a history of the mysterious lady, written 'by one of the race of Lusinia, William de Portenach, in Italian'. This history if it ever existed, has not come down to us; the work of Jean d'Arras is a complete romance. According to him, Helmas, king of Albania (Scotland, or, as the German popular versions have it, Nordland), married a fay named Pressina, whom he found singing beside a fountain. She became his, after having exacted from him an oath never to visit her during her lying-in. She gave birth to three little girls at once, Melusina, Melior, and Plantina. A son of Helmas by a former wife hurried to his father with the joyful news, and the king, oblivious of his promise, rushed to his wife and found her bathing her three children. Pressina, on seeing him, exclaimed against his forgetfulness, and, taking her babes in her arms, vanished. She brought up the daughters until they were fifteen, when she unfolded to them the story of their father's breach of promise, and Melusina, the youngest, determined on revenge. She, in concert with her sisters, caught King Helmas and chained him in the heart of a mountain called Avalon, or, in the German books, Brunbelois, in Northubelon, i.e. Northumberland. At this unfilial act, the mother was so indignant, that she sentenced her daughter Melusina to spend the sabbath in a semi-fish form, till she should marry one who would never inquire into what became of her on that day. Jean d'Arras relates that Serville, who defended Lusignan for the English against the Duke de Berry, swore to that prince upon his faith and honour, 'that three days before the surrender of the castle, there entered into his chamber, though the doors were shut, a large serpent, enamelled blue and white, which struck its tail several times against the foot of the bed whereon he was lying with his wife, who was not at all frightened at it, though he was very considerably so; and that when he seized his sword, the serpent changed all at once into a woman, and said to him: "How, Serville, you, who have been in so many battles and sieges, are you afraid? Know that I am the mistress of this castle, which I erected, and that soon you will have to surrender it!" When she had ended these words, she resumed her serpent-shape, and glided away so swiftly that he could not perceive her.'

Stephan, a Dominican, of the house of Lusignan, developed the work of Jean d'Arras, and made the story so famous, that the families of Luxembourg, Rohan, and Sassenaye altered their pedigrees so as to be able to claim descent from the illustrious Melusina; and the Emperor Henry VII felt no little pride in being able to number the beautiful and mysterious lady among his ancestors. 'It does not escape me,' writes the chronicler Conrad Vecerius, in his life of that emperor, 'to report what is related in a little work in the vernacular, concerning the acts of a woman, Melyssina, on one day of the week becoming a serpent from her middle downwards, whom they reckon among the ancestors of Henry VII. . . . But, as authors relate, that in a certain island of the ocean, there are nine Sirens endowed with various arts, such, for instance, as changing themselves into any shape they like, it is no absurd conjecture to suppose that Melyssina came thence.'

The story became immensely popular in France, in Germany, and in Spain, and was printed and reprinted. The following are some of the principal early editions of it.

Jean d'Arras, 'Le liure de Melusine en fracoys', Geneva, 1478. The same, Lyons and Paris, without date; Lyons, 4to, 1500, and again 1544; Troyes, 4to, no date. 'L'histoire de Melusine fille du roy d'Albanie et de dame Pressine, revue et mise en meilleur langage que par cy devant', Lyons, 1597. 'Le roman de Melusine, princesse de Lusignan, avec l'histoire de Geoffry, surnommé à la Grand Dent', par Nodot, Paris, 1700. An outline of the story in the 'Bibliothèque des Romans', 1775, T. II. A Spanish version, 'Historia de la linda Melosyna', Tolosa, 1489. 'La hystoria de la linda Melosina', Sevilla, 1526. A Dutch translation, 'Een san sonderlingke schone ende wonderlike historie, die men warachtich kout te syne ende autentick sprekende van eenre vrouwen gheheeten Melusine', Tantwerpen, 1500. A Bohemian version, probably translated from the German, 'Kronyke Kratochwilne, o ctné a slech netné Panně Meluzijně', Prag, 1760, 1764, 1805. A Danish version, made about 1579, 'Melusine', Copenhagen, 1667, 1702, 1729. One in Swedish, without date. The original of these three last was the 'History of Melusine', by Thüring von Ringoltingen, published in 1456; Augsburg, 1474; Strasburg, 1478. 'Melosine-Geschicht', illustrated with woodcuts, Heidelberg, 1491. 'Die Historia von Melusina', Strasburg, 1506. 'Die Histori oder Geschicht von der edle und schönen Melusina', Augsburg, 1547; Strasburg, 1577, 1624. 'Wunderbare Geschichte von der edeln und schönen Melusina, welche eine Tochter des Königs Helmus und ein Meerwunder gewesen ist', Nürnberg, without date; reprinted in Marbach's 'Volksbücher', Leipzig, 1838.

In the fable of Melusina, there are several points deserving of consideration, as – the framework of the story, the half-serpent or fish-shape of Melusina, and her appearances as warnings of impending misfortune or death. The minor details, as, for instance, the trick with the hide, which is taken from the story of Dido, shall not detain us.

The framework of the myth is the story-radical corresponding with that of Lohengrin. The skeleton of the romance is this –

1. A man falls in love with a woman of supernatural race.
2. She consents to live with him, subject to one condition.
3. He breaks the condition and loses her.
4. He seeks her, and – α. recovers her; β. never recovers her.

In the story before us, the last item has dropped out, but it exists in many other stories which have sprung from the same root. The beautiful legend of Undine is but another version of the same story. A young knight marries a water-sprite, and promises never to be false to her, and never to bring her near a river. He breaks his engagement, and loses her. Then she comes to him on the eve of his second marriage and kisses him to death. Fouqué's inimitable romance is founded on the story as told by Theophrastus Paracelsus in his 'Treatise on Elemental Sprites', but the bare bones of the myth related by the philosopher have been quickened into life and beauty by the heaven-drawn spark of poetry wherewith Fouqué has endowed them.

In the French tale, Melusina seeks union with a mortal solely that she may escape from her enchantment; but in the German more earnest tale, Undine desires to become a bride that she may obtain an immortal soul. The corresponding Danish story is told by Hans Christian Andersen. A little mermaid sees a prince as she floats on the surface of the sea, and saves him in her arms from drowning when the ship is wrecked. But from that hour her heart is filled with yearning love for the youth whose life she has preserved. She seeks earth of her own free will, leaving her native element, although the consequence is pain at every step she takes.

She becomes the constant attendant of the prince, till he marries a princess, when her heart breaks and she becomes a Light-Elf, with prospect of immortality.

Belonging to the same family is the pretty Indian tale of Urvaçî. Urvaçî was an 'apsaras', or heavenly maiden; she loved Puravaras, a martial king, and became his wife, only, however, on condition that she should never behold him without his clothes. For some years they were together, till the heavenly companions of Urvaçî determined to secure her return to her proper sphere. They accordingly beguiled Puravaras into leaving his bed in the darkness of night, and then, with a lightning-flash, they disclosed him in his nudity to the wife, who was thereupon constrained to leave him. A somewhat similar story is told, in the Katha Sarit Sagara, of Vidû-shaka, who loves and marries a beautiful Bhadrâ but after a while she vanishes, leaving behind her a ring. The inconsolable husband wanders in search of her, and reaching the heavenly land, drops the ring in a goblet of water, which is taken to her. By this she recognizes him, and they are re-united.

The legend of Melusina, as it comes to us, is by no means in its original condition. Jean d'Arras, or other romancers, have considerably altered the simple tale, so as to make it assume the proportions of a romance. All that story of the fay Pressina, and her marriage with King Helmas, is but another version of the same story as Melusina.

Helmas finds Pressina near a fountain, and asks her to be his; she consents on condition that he does not visit her during her lying-in; he breaks the condition and loses her. This is the same as Raymond discovering Melusina near a spring, and obtaining her hand subject to the condition that he will not visit her one day of the week. Like Helmas, he breaks his promise and loses his wife. That both Pressina and Melusina are water-sprites, or nymphs, is unquestionable; both haunt a fountain, and the transformation of the lady of Lusignan indicates her aquatic origin. As Grimm has observed, this is a Gallic, and therefore a Keltic myth, an opinion confirmed by the Banshee part played by the unfortunate nymph. For the Banshee superstition has no corresponding feature in Scandinavian, Teutonic, or Classic mythology, and belongs entirely to the Kelts. Among others there are death portents, but not, that I am aware of, spirits of women attached to families, by their bitter cries at night announcing the approach of the king of terrors.

The Irish Banshee is thus described: 'We saw the figure of a tall, thin woman with uncovered head, and long hair that floated round her shoulders, attired in something which seemed either a loose white cloak or a sheet thrown hastily about her, uttering piercing cries.

'The most remarkable instance (of the Banshee) occurs in the MS memoirs of Lady Fanshawe, so exemplary for her conjugal affection. Her husband, Sir Richard, and she chanced, during their abode in Ireland, to visit a friend, the head of a sept, who resided in an ancient baronial castle surrounded with a moat. At midnight she was awakened by a ghastly and supernatural scream, and looking out of bed, beheld in the moonlight a female face and part of the form hovering at the window. The face was that of a young and rather handsome woman, but pale, and the hair, which was reddish, loose and dishevelled. The dress, which Lady Fanshawe's terror did not prevent her remarking accurately, was that of the ancient Irish. This apparition continued to exhibit itself for some time, and then vanished, with two shrieks similar to that which had first excited Lady Fanshawe's attention. In the morning, with infinite terror, she communicated to her host what she had witnessed, and found him prepared, not only to credit, but to account for the apparition:–

"'A near relation of my family,' said he, 'expired last night in this castle. We disguised our certain expectations of the event from you, lest it should throw a cloud over the cheerful reception which was your due. Now, before such an event happens in this family and castle, the female spectre whom ye have seen always is visible: she is believed to be the spirit of a woman of inferior rank, whom one of my ancestors degraded himself by marrying, and whom afterwards, to expiate the dishonour done to his family, he caused to be drowned in the castle moat.'"

A very remarkable story of the Banshee is given by Mr Crofton Croker. The Rev. Charles Bunworth was rector of Buttevant, in the county Cork, about the middle of last century. He was famous for his performance on the national instrument, the Irish harp, and for his hospitable reception and entertainment of the poor harpers who travelled from house to house about the country; and in his granary were deposited fifteen harps, bequeathed to him by the last members of a race which has now ceased to exist.

The circumstances attending the death of Mr Bunworth were remarkable; but, says Mr Crofton Croker, there are still living credible witnesses who declare their authenticity, and who can be produced to attest most, if not all, of the following particulars. Shortly before his decease, a shepherd heard the Banshee keening and clapping her hands under a lightning-struck tree near the house. On the eve of his death the night was serene and moonlit, and nothing broke the stillness of the melancholy watch kept by the bedside of the sick man, who lay in the drawing-room, by his two daughters. The little party were suddenly roused by a sound at the window near the bed: a rose-tree grew outside the window, so closely as to touch the glass; this was forced aside with some noise, and a low moaning was heard, accompanied by clapping of hands, as if of some female in deep affliction. It seemed as if the sound proceeded from a person holding her mouth close to the window. The lady who sat by the bedside of Mr Bunworth went into the adjoining room, where sat some male relatives, and asked, in a tone of alarm, if they had heard the Banshee. Sceptical of supernatural appearances, two of them rose hastily, and went out to discover the cause of these sounds, which they also distinctly heard. They walked all round the house, examining every spot of ground, particularly near the window from whence the voice had proceeded; the bed of earth beneath, in which the rose-tree was planted, had been recently dug, and the print of a footstep – if the tree had been forced aside by mortal hand – would have inevitably remained; but they could perceive no such impression, and an unbroken stillness reigned without. Hoping to dispel the mystery, they continued their search anxiously along the road, from the straightness of which, and the lightness of the night, they were enabled to see some distance around them; but all was silent and deserted, and they returned surprised and disappointed. How much more then were they astonished at learning that, the whole time of their absence, those who remained within the house had heard the moaning and clapping of hands even louder and more distinct than before they had gone out; and no sooner was the door of the room closed on them, than they again heard the same mournful sounds. Every succeeding hour the sick man became worse, and when the first glimpse of the morning appeared, Mr Bunworth expired.

The Banshee is represented in Wales by the Gwrâch y Rhibyn, who is said to come after dusk, and flap her leathern wings against the window, giving warning of death, in a broken, howling tone, and calling on the one who is to quit mortality by his or her name several times. In Brittany, similar spirits are called Bandrhudes, and are attached to several of the ancient families. In other parts of France, they pass as Dames Blanches, who, however, are not to be confused with the Teutonic white ladies, which are spirits of a different order.

But, putting the Banshee part of the story of Melusina on one side, let us turn to the semi-fish or serpent form of Melusina. Jean d'Arras attributes this to a curse pronounced on her by the fay Pressina, but this is an invention of his own; the true conception of Melusina he did not grasp, and was therefore obliged to forge a legend which should account for her peculiar appearance. Melusina was a mermaid. Her presence beside the fountain, as well as her fishy tail, indicate her nature; she was not, perhaps, a native of the sea, but a stream-dweller, and therefore as closely related to the true mermaid of the briny deep as are the fresh-water fish to those of the salt sea.

The superstitious belief in mermaids is universal, and I frankly confess my inability to account for its origin in every case. In some particular cases the origin of the myth is clear, in others it is not so. Let me take one which can be explained – the Oannes of the Chaldæans, the Philistine Dagon.

Oannes and Dag-on (the fish On) are identical. According to an ancient fable preserved by Berosus, a creature half man and half fish came out of 'that part of the Erythræan sea which borders upon Babylonia', where he taught men the arts of life, 'to construct cities, to found temples, to compile laws, and, in short, instructed them in all things that tend to soften manners and humanize their lives'; and he adds that a representation of this animal Oannes was preserved in his day. A figure of him sporting in the waves, and apparently blessing a fleet of vessels, was discovered in a marine piece of sculpture, by M. Botta, in the excavation of Khorsabad.

At Nimroud, a gigantic image was found by Mr Layard, representing him with the fish's head as a cap and the body of the fish depending over his shoulders, his legs those of a man, in his left hand holding a richly decorated bag, and his right hand upraised, as if in the act of presenting the mystic Assyrian fir-cone.

This Oannes is the Mizraimite On, and the Hebrew Aon, with a Greek case-termination, derived from a root signifying 'to illumine'. Aon was the original name of the god reverenced in the temple of Heliopolis, which in Scripture is called Beth-Aon, the house of On, as well as by its translation Beth-Shemesh, the house of the Sun. Not only does his name indicate his solar origin, but his representation with horned head-dress testifies to his nature. Ammon, Apis, Dionysos are sun-gods; Isis, Io, Artemis are moon-goddesses, and are all horned. Indeed, in ancient iconography horns invariably connect the gods represented with the two great sources of light. Apparent exceptions, such as the Fauns, are not so in reality, when subjected to close scrutiny. Civilizing gods, who diffuse intelligence and instruct barbarians, are also solar deities, as the Egyptian Osiris, the Nabathæan Tammuz, the Greek Apollo, and the Mexican Quetzalcoatl; beside these Oannes takes his place, as the sun-god, giving knowledge and civilization. According to the fable related by Berosus, he came on earth each morning, and at evening plunged into the sea; this is a mythical description of the rising and setting of the sun. His semi-piscine form was an expression of the idea that half his time was spent above ground, and half below the waves.

In precisely similar manner the Semitic moon-goddess, who followed the course of the sun, at times manifesting herself to the eyes of men, at others seeking concealment in the western flood, was represented as half woman, half fish, with characteristics which make her lunar origin indisputable. Her name was Derceto or Atergatis. On the coins of Ascalon, where she was held in great honour, is figured a goddess above whose head is a half-moon, and at her feet a woman with her lower extremities like a fish. This is Semiramis, who, according to a popular legend, was the child of Derceto. At Joppa she appears as a mermaid. The story was, that she fled from Typhon, and plunged into the sea, concealing herself under the form of a fish. According to Plutarch, the Syrian Tirgata, the Derceto of Palestine, was the goddess of moisture; and Lucan declares that she was represented as a woman with a fish-tail from her hips downward.

In every mythology, the different attributes of the deity in process of time became distinct gods, yet with sufficient impress of their origin still upon them to make that origin easy to be detected.

As On, the sun-god rising and setting in the sea, was supplied with a corresponding moon-goddess, Atergatis, and Bel or Baal, also a solar deity, had his lunar Baalti, so the fiery Moloch, 'the great lord', was supplied with his Mylitta, 'the birth-producer'. Moloch was the fierce flame-god, and Mylitta the goddess of moisture. Their worship was closely united. The priests of Moloch wore female attire, the priestesses of Mylitta were dressed like men. Human sacrifices characterized the worship of the fire-god, prostitution that of the goddess of water. From her came the names of the hetaræ Melitta, Meleto, Milto, Milesia. Among the Carthaginians, this goddess was worshipped, as appears from their giving the name of Magasmelita (the tent of Mylitta) to one of the African provinces. Mylitta was identical with Atergatis; she was regarded as a universal mother, a source of life.

In Greece, the priestesses of Demeter were called Melissæ, the high-priest of Apollo was entitled *κύριος τῶν μελλισσῶν*. A fable was invented to account for this name, and to connect them with bees and honey; but I have little doubt that it was corrupted from the Semitic designation of the servants of Mylitta. The Melissæ are sometimes spoken of as nymphs, but are not to be identified with the Meliadæ, Dryads sprung from the ash. Yet Melia, daughter of Oceanus, who plunges into the Haliacmon, strongly resembles the Syrian goddess. Selene, the moon, was also known by the name Melissa. *Καὶ τὰς Δήμητρος ἱερείας, ὡς τῆς χθονίας θεᾶς μυστίδας, μελίσσας οἱ παλαιοὶ ἐκάλουν, αὐτήν τε τὴν Κόρην μελισσώδη, Σελήνην τε, οὖσαν γενέσεως προστατίδα μέλισσαν ἐκάλουν.*

When we remember the double character of Mylitta, as a generative or all-mother, and as a moon-goddess, we are able to account for her name having passed into the Greek titles of priestesses of their corresponding goddesses Demeter and Selene.

The name Melissa was probably introduced into Gaul by the Phocian colony at Massilia, the modern Marseilles, and passed into the popular mythology of the Gallic Kelts as the title of nymphs, till it was finally appropriated by the Melusina of romance.

It may seem difficult at first sight to trace the connexion between the moon, a water-goddess, and a deity presiding over childbirth; yet it is certain that such a connexion does exist. The classic Venus was born of the sea-foam, and was unmistakably one with the moon. She was also the goddess of love, and was resorted to by barren women – as the Venus of Quimperle in Brittany is, to this day, sought by those who have no children.

On the Syrian coast, they told of their goddess plunging into the sea, because they saw the moon descend into the western waters; but the Cretans, who beheld her rise above the eastern horizon of sea, fabled of a foam-born goddess.

In classic iconography the Tritons, and in later art the Sirens, are represented half fish, half human. Originally the Sirens were winged, but after the fable had been accepted, which told of their strife with the Muses, and their precipitation into the sea, they were figured like mermaids; the fish-form was by them borrowed from Derceto. It is curious how widely-spread is the belief in fish-women. The prevalence of tales of mermaids among Celtic populations indicates these water-nymphs as having been originally deities of those peoples; and I cannot but believe that the circular mirror they are usually represented as holding is a reminiscence of the moon-disk. Bothe, in his 'Kronecke der Sassen', in 1492, described a god, Krodo, worshipped in the Hartz, who was represented with his feet on a fish, a wheel to symbolize the moon in one hand, and a pail of water in the other. As among the Northern nations the moon is masculine, its deity was male. Probably the Mexican Coxcox or Teocipactli (i.e. Fish-god) was either a solar or lunar deity. He was entitled Huehueton-acateo-cateo-cipatli, or Fish-god-of-our-flesh, to give him his name in full; he somewhat resembled the Noah of Sacred Writ; for the Mexican fable related, that in a great time of flood, when the earth was covered with water, he rescued himself in a cypress trunk, and peopled the world with wise and intelligent beings. The Babylonish Oannes was also identified with the flood.

The Peruvians had likewise their semi-fish gods, but the legend connected with them has not descended to our days.

The North-American Indians relate that they were conducted from Northern Asia by a man-fish. 'Once upon a time, in the season of opening buds, the people of our nation were much terrified at seeing a strange creature, much resembling a man, riding upon the waves. He had upon his head long green hair, much resembling the coarse weeds which the mighty storms scatter along the margin of the strand. Upon his face, which was shaped like that of a porpoise, he had a beard of the same colour. But if our people were frightened at seeing a man who could live in the water like a fish or a duck, how much more were they frightened when they saw that from his breast down he was actually a fish, or rather two fishes, for each of his legs was a whole and distinct fish. And there he would sit for hours singing to the wondering ears of the Indians the beautiful things he saw in the depths of the ocean, always closing his strange stories with these words:– "Follow me, and see what I will show you." For a great many suns, they dared not venture upon the water; but when they grew hungry, they at last put to sea, and following the man-fish, who kept close to the boat, reached the American coast.'

It is not impossible that the North-American Indians may have symbolized the sun in the same manner as the Syrians, and that this legend may signify that the early colonists, to reach the New Land, followed the *fish*-course of the sun, which as man goes from East to West, whereas when it dives it swims from West to East, the course taken by the Indians in their canoes. The wanderers in the Canadian forests have also their fish-woman, of whom a tale is related which bears a lively resemblance to that of Undine, and which is not a little like that of Melusina.

One day an Ottawa chief, whilst sitting by the water side, beheld a beautiful woman rise from the flood, her face exquisitely lovely, her eyes blue, her teeth white, and her locks floating over her shoulders. From her waist downwards she was fish, or rather two fishes. She entreated the warrior to permit her to live on earth, as she desired to win a human soul, which could only be acquired by union with a mortal. He consented and took her to his house, where she was to him as a daughter. Some years after an Andirondack youth beheld and loved her. He took her to wife, and she obtained that which she had desired – a human soul.

In the Undine story, a water-maiden, in like manner and for a like object, is adopted by an old fisherman, and becomes the bride of a youthful German knight. But the Andirondack tribe was ill-pleased at the marriage of their chief with the mysterious damsel, and they tore her from his arms, and drove her back to her original element. Then all the water-spirits vowed revenge at the insult offered to one of their race; they stirred up war between the Ottawas and Andirondacks, which led to the extermination of the latter; one only was rescued, and he was grasped by the fish-wife, and by her borne down to the watery depths below the Falls of S. Anthony. In the German story, the husband is weary with the taunts of those around at having married a water-sprite, and bids her return to her element. Then the spirits of the flood vow his destruction, and send Undine on earth to embrace her faithless lord, and kiss him to death. The name of the fish-woman is in German Meerfrau or Meriminni; in Danish, the Siren is Maremind; and in Icelandic and old Norse, Marmennill; in Irish she is the Merrow; with the Breton peasantry she is Marie-Morgan. In the legendary lore of all these people, there are stories of the loves of a mortal man and a mermaid. According to Mr Crofton Croker, O'Sullivan More, Lord of Dunkerron, lost his heart to one of these beautiful water-sprites, and she agreed to be his, but her parents resented the union and killed her.

On the shore of Smerwick harbour, an Irishman, Dick Fitzgerald, caught a Merrow with her *cohuleen driuth*, or enchanted cap, lying on a rock beside her. He grasped the cap, and thereby possessed himself of the nymph, who, however, seemed nothing loth to obtain a mortal husband. They lived together happily for some years, and saw a family of beautiful children grow up at their knees. But one day the Lady of Gollerus, as she was called, discovered her old cap in a corner. She took it up and looked at it, and then thought of her father the king and her mother the queen, and felt a longing to go back to them. She kissed the babies, and then went down to the strand with the full intention of returning to Gollerus after a brief visit to her home. However, no sooner was the *cohuleen driuth* on her head, than all remembrance of her life on earth was forgotten, and she plunged into the sea, never to return. Similar tales are related in Shetland, the Faroes, in Iceland, and Norway.

Vade, the father of the famous smith Velund, was the son of King Vilkin and a mermaid whom he met in a wood on the sea-shore in Russia. In the Saga of Half and his knights is an account of a merman who was caught and kept a little while on land. He sang the following entreaty to be taken back to his native element –

'Cold water to the eyes!
Flesh raw to the teeth!
A shroud to the dead!
Flit me back to the sea!

Henceforward never
Men in ships sailing!
Draw me to dry land
From the depth of the sea!'

In the 'Speculum Regale', an Icelandic work of the twelfth century, is the following description of a mermaid:–

'A monster is seen also near Greenland, which people call the Margygr. This creature appears like a woman as far down as her waist, with breast and bosom like a woman, long hands, and soft hair, the neck and head in all respects like those of a human being. The hands seem to people to be long, and the fingers not to be parted, but united by a web like that on the feet of water birds. From the waist downwards, this monster resembles a fish, with scales, tail, and fins. This prodigy is believed to show itself especially before heavy storms. The habit of this creature is to dive frequently and rise again to the surface with fishes in its hands. When sailors see it playing with the fish, or throwing them towards the ship, they fear that they are doomed to lose several of the crew; but when it casts the fish, or, turning from the vessel, flings them away from her, then the sailors take it as a good omen that they will not suffer loss in the impending storm. This monster has a very horrible face, with broad brow and piercing eyes, a wide mouth, and double chin.' The Landnama, or Icelandic Doomsday book, speaks of a Marmennill, or merman, having been caught off the island of Grimsey; and the annals of the same country relate the appearance of these beings off the coast in 1305 and in 1329.

Megasthenes reported that the sea which washed Taprobane, the modern Ceylon, was inhabited by a creature having the appearance of a woman; and Ælian improved this account, by stating that there are whales having the form of Satyrs. In 1187, a merman was fished up off the coast of Suffolk. It closely resembled a man, but was not gifted with speech. One day, when it had the opportunity to escape, it fled to the sea, plunged in, and was never seen again. Pontoppidan records the appearance of a merman, which was deposed to on oath by the observers.

'About a mile from the coast of Denmark, near Landscrona, three sailors, observing something like a dead body floating in the water, rowed towards it. When they came within seven or eight fathoms, it still appeared as at first, for it had not stirred; but at that instant it sank, and came up almost immediately in the same place. Upon this, out of fear, they lay still, and then let the boat float, that they might the better examine the monster, which, by the help of the current, came nearer and nearer to them. He turned his face and stared at them, which gave them a good opportunity of examining him narrowly. He stood in the same place for seven or eight minutes, and was seen above the water breast-high. At last they grew apprehensive of some danger, and began to retire; upon which the monster blew up his cheeks and made a kind of lowing noise, and then dived from their view. In regard to his form, they declare in their affidavits, which were regularly taken and recorded, that he appeared like an old man, strong limbed, with broad shoulders, but his arms they could not see. His head was small in proportion to his body, and had short, curled black hair, which did not reach below his ears; his eyes lay deep in his head, and he had a meagre face, with a black beard; about the body downwards, this merman was quite pointed like a fish.'

In the year 1430, after a violent tempest, which broke down the dykes in Holland and flooded the low lands, some girls of the town of Edam in West Friesland, going in a boat to milk their cows, observed a mermaid in shallow water and embarrassed in the mud.

They took it into their boat and brought it into Edam, dressed it in female attire, and taught it to spin. It fed with them, but never could be taught to speak. It was afterwards brought to Haerlem, where it lived for several years, though still showing a strong inclination for water. Parival, in his 'Délices de Hollande', relates that it was instructed in its duty to God, and that it made reverences before a crucifix. Old Hudson, the navigator, in his dry and ponderous narrative, records the following incident, when trying to force a passage to the pole near Nova Zembla, lat. 75°, on the 15th June. 'This morning, one of our company looking overboard saw a mermaid; and calling up some of the company to see her, one more came up, and by that time she was come close to the ship's side, looking earnestly at the men. A little after, a sea came and overturned her. From the navel upward, her back and breasts were like a woman's, as they say that saw her; her body as big as one of us, her skin very white, and long hair hanging down behind, of colour black. In her going down they saw her tail, which was like the tail of a porpoise, speckled like a mackerel. Their names that saw her were Thomas Hilles and Robert Rayner.'

In 1560, near the island of Mandar, on the west of Ceylon, some fishermen entrapped in their net seven mermen and mermaids, of which several Jesuits, and Father Henriques, and Bosquez, physician to the Viceroy of Goa, were witnesses. The physician examined them with a great deal of care, and dissected them. He asserts that the internal and external structure resembled that of human beings. We have another account of a merman seen near the great rock Diamon, on the coast of Martinique. The persons who saw it gave a precise description of it before a notary; they affirmed that they saw it wipe its hands over its face, and even heard it blow its nose. Another creature of the same species was captured in the Baltic in 1531, and sent as a present to Sigismund, King of Poland, with whom it lived three days, and was seen by all the Court. Another was taken near Rocca de Sintra, as related by Damian Goes. The King of Portugal and the Grand-Master of the Order of S. James are said to have had a suit at law, to determine which party the creature belonged to.

Captain Weddell, well known for his geographical discoveries in the extreme south of the globe, relates the following story:– 'A boat's crew were employed on Hall's Island, when one of the crew, left to take care of some produce, saw an animal whose voice was even musical. The sailor had lain down, and about ten o'clock he heard a noise resembling human cries; and as daylight in these latitudes never disappears at this season, he rose and looked around, but, on seeing no person, returned to bed. Presently he heard the noise again, rose a second time, but still saw nothing. Conceiving, however, the possibility of a boat being upset, and that some of the crew might be clinging to some detached rocks, he walked along the beach a few steps, and heard the noise more distinctly, but in a musical strain. Upon searching round, he saw an object lying on a rock a dozen yards from the shore, at which he was somewhat frightened. The face and shoulders appeared of human form, and of a reddish colour; over the shoulders hung long green hair; the tail resembled that of the seal, but the extremities of the arms he could not see distinctly. The creature continued to make a musical noise while he gazed about two minutes, and on perceiving him it disappeared in an instant. Immediately when the man saw his officer, he told this wild tale, and to add weight to his testimony (being a Romanist) he made a cross on the sand, which he kissed, as making oath to the truth of his statement. When I saw him, he told the story in so clear and positive a manner, making oath to its truth, that I concluded he must really have seen the animal he described, or that it must have been the effect of a disturbed imagination.'

In a splendidly illustrated work with plates coloured by hand, 'Poissons, écrevisses et crabes de diverses couleurs et figures extraordinaires, que l'on trouve autour des Isles Moluques', dedicated to King George of England, and published by Louis Renard at Amsterdam, in 1717, is a curious account of a mermaid. This book was the result of thirty years' labour, in the Indian seas, by Blatazar Coyett, Governor of the Islands of the Province of Amboine and President of the Commissioners in Batavia, and by Adrien Van der Stell, Governor Regent of the Province of Amboine. In the 2nd volume, p. 240, is the picture of a mermaid . . . and the subjoined description:–

'See-wyf. A monster resembling a Siren, caught near the island of Borné, or Boeren, in the Department of Amboine. It was 59 inches long, and in proportion as an eel. It lived on land, in a vat full of water, during four days seven hours. From time to time it uttered little cries like those of a mouse. It would not eat, though it was offered small fish, shells, crabs, lobsters, &c. After its death, some excrement was discovered in the vat, like the secretion of a cat.' The copy . . . I have [used] is thus coloured: hair, the hue of kelp; body, olive tint; webbed olive between the fingers, which have each four joints; the fringe round the waist orange, with a blue border; the fins green, face slate-grey; a delicate row of pink hairs runs the length of the tail.

With such a portrait we may well ask with Tennyson–

> Who would be
> A mermaid fair,
> Singing alone,
> Combing her hair
> Under the sea
> In a golden curl,
> With a comb of pearl,
> On a throne?

The introduction to the book contains additional information.

The *Avertissement de l'Editeur* says:– 'M. Baltazar Coyett is the first to whom the great discovery is due. Whilst governor, he encouraged the fishery of these fishes; and after having had about two hundred painted of those which were brought to his home by the Indians of Amboine and the neighbouring isles, as well as by the Dutch there settled, he formed of them two collections, the originals of which were brought by his son to M. Scott the Elder, who was then chief advocate, or prime minister, of the Company General of the East Indies at Amsterdam. He had them copied exactly. The second volume, *less correct* indeed in the exactitude of the drawings, but very curious on account of the novelties wherewith it is filled, and of the remarks accompanying each fish, was taken from the collection of M. Van der Stell, Governor of the Moluccas, by a painter named Gamael Fallours, who brought them to me from the Indies, and of which I have selected about 250. Moreover, to check incredulity in certain persons, I have thought fit to subjoin the following certificates.' Among them, the most curious are those relating to the mermaid.

Letter from Renard, the publisher, to M. François Valentyn, minister of the Gospel at Dort, late superintendent of the churches in the colonies, dated Amsterdam, Dec. 17, 1716.

Monsieur,

His Majesty the Czar of Muscovy having done me the honour of visiting my house, and having had occasion to show the prince the work on the fishes of the Molucca islands, by the Sieur Fallours, in which, among other drawings, is the enclosed plate, representing a monster resembling a Siren, which this painter says that he saw alive for four days at Amboine, as you will be pleased to see in the writing with his own hand, which accompanies this picture, and as he believes that M. Van der Stell, the present Governor of Amboine, may have sent it to you, I remarked that his Majesty the Czar would be much gratified to have this fact substantiated; wherefore I shall be greatly obliged if you will favour me with a reply.

I remain, &c.

REPLY

DORT, Dec. 18, 1716.

Monsieur,

It is not impossible that, since my departure from the Indies, Fallours may have seen at Amboine the monster whose picture you had the courtesy to send me, and which I return enclosed; but up to the present moment I have neither seen nor heard of the original. If I had the creature, I would with all my heart make a present of it to his Majesty the Czar, whose application in the research of objects of curiosity deserves the praise of all the world. But, sir, as evidence that there are monsters in nature resembling this Siren, I may say that I know for certain, that in the year 1652 or 1653 a lieutenant in the service of the Company saw two of these beings in the gulf, near the village of Hennetelo, near the islands of Ceram and Bœro, in the Department of Amboine. They were swimming side by side, which made him presume that one was male, the other female. Six weeks after they reappeared in the same spot, and were seen by more than fifty persons. These monsters were of a greenish grey colour, having precisely the shape of human beings from the head to the waist, with arms and hands, but their bodies tapered away. One was larger than the other; their hair was moderately long. I may add that, on my way back from the Indies, in which I resided thirty years, I saw, on the 1st May, 1714, long. 12° 18′, and on the Meridian, during clear, calm weather, at the distance of three or four ship-lengths off, a monster, which was apparently a sort of marine-man, of a bluish grey (gris de mer). It was raised well above the surface, and seemed to have a sort of fisher's cap of moss on its head. All the ship's company saw it, as well as myself; but although its back was turned towards us, the monster seemed conscious that we were approaching too near, and it dived suddenly under water, and we saw it no more.

I am, &c.,

F. VALENTYN

Letter from M. Parent, Pastor of the church of Amsterdam, written and exhibited before the notary Jacob Lansman.

AMSTERDAM, July 15, 1717.

Monsieur,

I have seen with mingled pleasure and surprise the illuminated proofs of the beautiful plates which you have had engraved, representing the fishes of Molucca, which were painted from nature by the Sieur Samuel Fallours, with whom I was acquainted when at Amboine. I own, sir, that I was struck with astonishment at the sight of this work, the engravings of which closely resemble the fishes I have seen during my life, and which, or some of which, I have had the pleasure of eating during the thirteen years I resided at Amboine, from which I returned with the fleet in 1716. ... Touching your inquiry, whether I ever saw a Siren in that country, I reply that, whilst making the circuit of our churches in the Molucca Isles (which is done twice in the year by the pastors who understand the language of the country), and navigating in an *orambay*, or species of galley, between the villages of Holilieuw and Karieuw, distant from one another about two leagues by water, it happened, whilst I was dozing, that the negro rowers uttered a shrill cry of astonishment, which aroused me with a start; and when I inquired the cause of their outcry, they replied unanimously that they had seen clearly and distinctly a monster like a Siren, with a face resembling that of a man, and long hair like that of a woman floating down its back; but at their cry it had replunged into the sea, and all I could see was the agitation of the water where this Siren had disturbed it by diving.

I am, sir, &c.,

PARENT

One of the most remarkable accounts of a mermaid is that in Dr Robert Hamilton's 'History of the Whales and Seals', in the 'Naturalist's Library', he himself vouching for its general truth, from personal knowledge of some of the parties. 'It was reported that a fishing-boat off the island of Yell, one of the Shetland group, had captured a mermaid by its getting entangled in the lines.' The statement is, that the animal was about three feet long, the upper part of the body resembling the human, with protuberant mammæ, like a woman; the face, the forehead, and neck were short, and resembling those of a monkey; the arms, which were small, were kept folded across the breast; the fingers were distinct, not webbed; a few stiff, long bristles were on the top of the head, extending down to the shoulders, and these it could erect and depress at pleasure, something like a crest. The inferior part of the body was like a fish. The skin was smooth, and of a grey colour. It offered no resistance, nor attempted to bite, but uttered a low, plaintive sound. The crew, six in number, took it within their boat; but superstition getting the better of curiosity, they carefully disentangled it from the lines and from a hook which had accidentally fastened in its body, and returned it to its native element. It instantly dived, descending in a perpendicular direction.

'After writing the above, (we are informed) the narrator had an interview with the skipper of the boat and one of the crew, from whom he learned the following additional particulars. They had the animal for three hours within the boat; the body was without scales or hair, was of a silver-grey colour above and white below, like the human skin; no gills were observed, nor fins on the back or belly; the tail was like that of the dog-fish; the mammæ were about as large as those of a woman; the mouth and lips were very distinct, and resembled the human. This communication was from Mr Edmonton, a well-known and intelligent observer, to the distinguished professor of natural history in the Edinburgh University; and Mr E. adds a few reflections, which are so pertinent that we shall avail ourselves of them. That a very peculiar animal has been taken, no one can doubt. It was seen and handled by six men on one occasion and for some time, not one of whom dreams of a doubt of its being a mermaid. If it were supposed that their fears magnified its supposed resemblance to the human form, it must at all events be admitted that there was some ground for exciting these fears. But no such fears were likely to be entertained; for the mermaid is not an object of terror to the fisherman: it is rather a welcome guest, and danger is to be apprehended only from its experiencing bad treatment. The usual resources of scepticism, that the seals and other sea-animals, appearing under certain circumstances, operating on an excited imagination, and so producing ocular illusion cannot avail here. It is quite impossible that, under the circumstances, six Shetland fishermen could commit such a mistake.'

One of these creatures was found in the belly of a shark, on the north-west coast of Iceland, and is thus described by Wernhard Guthmund's son, priest of Ottrardale:–

'The lower part of the animal was entirely eaten away, whilst the upper part, from the epigastric and hypogastric region, was in some places partially eaten, in others completely devoured. The sternum, or breast-bone, was perfect. This animal appeared to be about the size of a boy eight or nine years old, and its head was formed like that of a man. The anterior surface of the occiput was very protuberant, and the nape of the neck had a considerable indentation or sinking. The alæ of the ears were very large, and extended a good way back. It had front teeth, which were long and pointed, as were also the larger teeth. The eyes were lustreless, and resembled those of a codfish. It had on its head long black, coarse hair, very similar to the *fucus filiformis*; this hair hung over the shoulders. Its forehead was large and round. The skin above the eyelids was much wrinkled, scanty, and of a bright olive colour, which was indeed the hue of the whole body. The chin was cloven, the shoulders were high, and the neck uncommonly short. The arms were of their natural size, and each hand had a thumb and four fingers covered with flesh. Its breast was formed exactly like that of a man, and there was also to be seen something like nipples; the back was also like that of a man. It had very cartilaginous ribs; and in parts where the skin had been rubbed off, a black, coarse flesh was perceptible, very similar to that of the seal. This animal, after having been exposed about a week on the shore, was again thrown into the sea.'

To the manufactured mermaids which come from Japan, and which are exhibited at shows, it is not necessary to do more than allude; they testify to the Japanese conception of a sea-creature resembling the Tritons of ancient Greece, the Syrian On and Derceto, the Scandinavian Marmennill, and the Mexican Coxcox.

CHAPTER 9

The Fortunate Isles

T SEEMS that people have been seeking 'Lands to the West' for as long as recorded history. From the classical Greek accounts of Ogygia, Heliconia, or Atlantis to the Irish Land-Beyond-the-Wave or Tir fa Thon, virtually every major cultural area in the world has its stories of voyages to the Uttermost West in search of some paradisal realm. This theme was touched upon in the account of the Terrestrial Paradise (Chapter 7); the quest for the Fortunate Isles ultimately derives from the same need – which is to believe in a realm *on* this earth though not *of* it to which the souls of the departed find their way and where they are assured of a joyful and endlessly extended life. It is this desire which ultimately gave rise to the Christian myths of Heaven – though it is notable that in most of the other traditions mentioned below there is no belief in a negative afterlife like the Christian Hell. The Otherworld is, largely, a place of joy and self-fulfilment, a land where the Ancestors, the Great Dead, await us, and where we may expect to be cared for eternally.

At one time Britain itself was widely believed to be the place to which souls passed at death – until it became better known, that is, at which time the islands off the coast replaced the larger land mass as appropriate sites. This belief must have been substantiated by the number of burials which took place on the northernmost islands. Thus the Orkneys in particular were a graveyard for many native Britons, and it is still impossible to walk more than a few hundred metres on any of the main islands in the group without stumbling upon the remains of a grave mound. Similarly, Procopius wrote of the tradition of the dead being ferried from Cornwall to Brittany by fishermen who are suborned by spirits to act as substitute Charons. The same tradition is instanced in Brittany with the direction reversed.

Gould's remarks concerning the Celtic origins of the Isles of the Blest derive from extremely corrupt and inaccurate sources and should be largely ignored. His reference

96

to what he calls 'The Booty of the Deep', by the sixth-century bard Taliesin, is in fact a ninth-century poem called *The Spoils of Annwn* (that is, the Otherworld, or more precisely the 'In-World') which describes the journey undertaken by the hero Arthur and his warriors to the Otherworld in search of the Cauldron of Annwn, which could restore the dead to life. This is a precursor of the Grail quest but it specifically describes the voyage to seven islands, on each of which stands a fortress guarded by dreadful warriors. 'It was hard to converse with their leader', reads a line of the poem.

In this we very clearly have a description of a voyage by the living to the Otherworld. Generally it was necessary to have a guide who knew the way. One such, mentioned in Celtic tradition, is Barinthus, a living man who yet knew the ways of the stars and planets and could guide those who wished to go there to the lands of the dead. In Geoffrey of Monmouth's twelfth-century poem *The Life of Merlin* we read a very different account of the passing of Arthur in which, after the battle of Camlan, Taliesin, assisted by Barinthus, takes the wounded king to the Blessed Isles. Geoffrey, drawing upon ancient sources, gives the following description of the Fortunate Isles:

> The Island of Apples which men call 'The Fortunate Isle' gets its name from the fact because it produces all things of itself; the fields there have no need of the ploughs of the farmers and all cultivation is lacking except that which nature provides. Of its own accord it produces grain and grapes, and apple trees grow in its woods from the close-clipped grass. The ground of its own accord produces everything instead of merely grass, and people live there a hundred years or more.
>
> (translated by J. J. Parry)

This is very much the same place to which Ogier le Danois found himself beguiled by Fata Morgana (see below) or where Brendan the Voyager sailed with his crew in search of the Blessed Isles. The fact that he may well have discovered the continent of America has been well attested for a long while – as, indeed, has a more widespread Celtic presence in North America. The Celtic monks were certainly intrepid sailors, and are known to have reached Greenland and possibly Nova Scotia at least a hundred years before Columbus.

Another notable – though still little-known – explorer is Henry Sinclair, who was the Earl of Orkney from 1397 until his death in 1400. An account of his transatlantic voyage is to be read in the much debated Zeno Manuscript which purports to be an account, by the Italian sailor Antonio Zen, of his adventurous journey with Sinclair (whom he calls 'Zichmni', the nearest he could get to writing the Earl's proper name) to the country of Estotiland and Engroneland. A map of the places described in the Manuscript is now acknowledged to be far more accurate than most such medieval productions, and includes a clearly recognizable outline of the east coast of America. Sinclair, and those who followed in his footsteps, were seeking Lands to the West, and found them. Although these were not the Otherworlds for which earlier accounts had prepared them, they were every bit as wonderful and rich as they could have wished.

* * *

IN MY article on the 'Terrestrial Paradise', I mentioned the principal mediæval fables existing relative to that blessed spot, which was located, according to popular belief, in the remote East of Asia. The Ancients had a floating tradition relative to a vast continent called Atlantis, in the far West, where lay Kronos asleep, guarded by Briareus; a land of rivers, and woods, and soft airs, occupying in their thoughts the position assumed in Christian belief by the earthly paradise. The Fathers of the Church waged war against this object of popular mythology, for Scripture plainly indicated the position of the garden land as 'eastward in Eden'; but, notwithstanding their attempts to drive the western paradise from the minds of men, it held its ground, and was believed in throughout the middle ages, till Christopher Columbus sought and found Atlantis and paradise in the new world, a world in which the theories of the Ancients and of the Mediævals met, for it was truly east of Asia and west of Europe. 'The saintly theologians and philosophers were right,' are the words of the great admiral in one of his letters, 'when they fixed the site of the terrestrial paradise in the extreme Orient, because it is a most temperate clime; and the lands which I have just discovered are the limits of the Orient', an opinion he repeats in his letter of 1498: 'I am convinced that there is the terrestrial paradise', namely that which had been located by SS. Ambrose, Isidore, and the Venerable Bede in the East.

The belief in a western land, or group of islands, was prevalent among the Kelts as well as the Greek and Latin geographers, and was with them an article of religion, upon which were founded superstitious practices, which perpetuated themselves after the introduction of Christianity.

This belief in a western land probably arose from the discovery of objects, unfamiliar and foreign, washed up on the European shores. In the life of Columbus, Martin Vincent, pilot of the King of Portugal, picked up off Cape S. Vincent a piece of carved wood; and a similar fragment was washed ashore on the Island of Madeira, and found by Pedro Correa, brother-in-law of the great navigator. The inhabitants of the Azores said that when the wind blew from the West, there were brought ashore great bamboos and pines of a description wholly unknown to them. On the sands of the Island of Flores were found one day the bodies of two men with large faces, and with features very different from those of Europeans. On another occasion, two canoes were driven on the coast filled with strange men. In 1682, a Greenland canoe appeared off the Isle of Eda in the Orkneys, and in the church of Burra was long preserved an Esquimaux boat which had been washed ashore. On the stormy coast of the Hebrides are often found nuts, which are made by the fishermen into snuff-boxes or worn as amulets. Martin, who wrote of the Western Isles in 1703, calls them 'Molluka beans'. They are seeds of the *Mimosa scandens*, washed by the gulf-stream across the Atlantic to our shores. Great logs of drift-wood of a strange character are also carried to the same coasts, and are used by the islanders in the construction of their hovels.

In 1508, a French vessel met with a boat full of American Indians not far off the English coast, as Bembo tells us in his history of Venice. Other instances have been cited by commentators on the curious fragment of Cornelius Nepos, which gave rise in the middle ages to a discussion of the possibility of forcing a north-west passage to India. Humboldt, in his remarks on this passage, says: 'Pomponius Mela, who lived at a period sufficiently near that of Cornelius Nepos, relates, and Pliny repeats it, that Metellus Celer, whilst Proconsul of Gaul, received as a gift from a king of the Boii or Boeti (the name is somewhat uncertain, and Pliny calls him a king of the

Suevi) some Indians who, driven by the tempests from the Indian seas, landed on the coasts of Germany. It is of no importance discussing here whether Metellus Celer is the same as the Prætor of Rome in the year of the consulship of Cicero, and afterwards consul conjointly with L. Africanus; or whether the German king was Ariovistus, conquered by Julius Cæsar. What is certain is, that from the chain of ideas which lead Mela to cite this fact as indisputable, one may conclude that in his time it was believed in Rome that these swarthy men sent from Germany into Gaul had come across the ocean which bathes the East and North of Asia.'

The canoes, bodies, timber, and nuts, washed up on the western coasts of Europe, may have originated the belief in there being a land beyond the setting sun; and this country, when once supposed to exist, was variously designated as Meropis, the continent of Kronos, Ogygia, Atlantis, the Fortunate Isles, or the Garden of the Hesperides. Strabo says distinctly that the only hindrance in the way of passing west from Iberia to India is the vastness of the Atlantic ocean, but that 'in the same temperate zone as we inhabit, and especially about the parallel passing through Thinæ and traversing the Atlantic, there may exist two inhabited countries, and perhaps even more than two.' A more distinct prophecy of America than the vague expressions of Seneca – 'Finitam cuique rei magnitudinem natura dederat, dedit et modum: nihil infinitum est nisi Oceanus. Fertiles in Oceano jacere terras, ultraque Oceanum rursus alia littora, alium nasci orbem, nec usquam naturam rerum desinere, sed semper inde ubi desiisse videatur, novam exsurgere, facile ista finguntur, quia Oceanus navigari non potest.' Aristotle accepted the notion of there being a new continent in the West, and described it, from the accounts of the Carthaginians, as a land opposite the Pillars of Hercules (Str. of Gibraltar), fertile, well-watered, and covered with forests. Diodorus gives the Phœnicians the credit of having discovered it, and adds that there are lofty mountains in that country, and that the temperature is not subject to violent changes. He however tries to distinguish between it and the Elysium of Homer, the Fortunate Isles of Pindar, and the Garden of the Hesperides. The Carthaginians began to found colonies there, but were forbidden by law, as it was feared that the old mother settlement would be deserted for the new and more attractive country. Plutarch locates Homer's Island of Ogygia five days' sail to the west of Brittia, and he adds, the great continent, or terra firma, is five thousand stadia from Ogygia. It stretches far away towards the north, and the people inhabiting this great land regard the old world as a small island. This is an observation made also by Theopompus, in his geographical myth of Meropis.

The ancient theories of Atlantis shall detain us no longer, as they have been carefully and exhaustively treated by Humboldt in the already quoted work on the geography of the New World. We shall therefore pass to the Kelts, and learn the position occupied by America in their mythology.

Brittia, says Procopius, lies 200 stadia from the coast between Britannia and Thule, opposite the mouth of the Rhine, and is inhabited by Angles, Frisians, and Britons. By Britannia he means the present Brittany, and Brittia is England. Tzetze relates that on the ocean coast, opposite Britannia, live fishermen subject to the Franks, but freed from paying tribute, on account of their occupation, which consists in rowing souls across to the opposite coast. Procopius tells the same story, and Sir Walter Scott gives it from him in his 'Count Robert of Paris'. 'I have read,' says Agelastes, 'in that brilliant mirror which reflects the times of our fathers, the volumes of the learned Procopius, that beyond Gaul, and nearly opposite to it, but separated by an arm of

the sea, lies a ghastly region, on which clouds and tempests for ever rest, and which is known to its continental neighbours as the abode to which departed spirits are sent after this life. On one side of the strait dwell a few fishermen, men possessed of a strange character, and enjoying singular privileges in consideration of thus being the living ferrymen who, performing the office of the heathen Charon, carry the spirits of the departed to the island which is their residence after death. At the dead of the night these fishermen are in rotation summoned to perform the duty by which they seem to hold permission to reside on this strange coast. A knock is heard at the door of his cottage, who holds the turn of this singular office, founded by no mortal hand; a whispering, as of a decaying breeze, summons the ferryman to his duty. He hastens to his bark on the sea-shore, and has no sooner launched it, than he perceives its hull sink sensibly in the water, so as to express the weight of the dead with whom it is filled. No form is seen; and though voices are heard, yet the accents are undistinguishable, as of one who speaks in his sleep.' According to Villemarqué, the place whence the boat put off with its ghostly freight was near Raz, a headland near the Bay of Souls, in the extreme west of Finisterre. The bare, desolate valleys of this cape, opposite the Island of Seint, with its tarn of Kleden, around which dance nightly the skeletons of drowned mariners, the abyss of Plogoff, and the wild moors studded with Druid monuments, make it a scene most suitable for the assembly of the souls previous to their ghastly voyage. Here, too, in Yawdet, the ruins of an ancient town near Llannion, has been identified the 'Γάδετοι of Strabo'.

'On the great island of Brittia,' continues Procopius, 'the men of olden time built a great wall cutting off a great portion of the land. East of this wall, there was a good climate and abundant crops, but west of it, on the contrary, it was such that no man could live there an hour; it was the haunt of myriads of serpents and other reptiles and if any one crossed the wall, he died at once, poisoned by the noxious exhalations.' This belief, which acted as a second wall to the realm of the dead, preserved strict privacy for the spirits. Procopius declares that this tradition was widely spread, and that it was reported to him by many people.

Claudian also heard of the same myth, but confused it with that of the nether world of Odysseus. 'At the extreme coast of Gaul is a spot protected from the tides of Ocean, where Odysseus by bloodshed allured forth the silent folk. There are heard wailing cries, and the light fluttering around of the shadows. And the natives there see pale, statue-like figures and dead corpses wandering.' According to Philemon in Pliny, the Cimbri called the Northern Ocean Morimarusa, *i.e.* mare mortuum, the sea of the dead.

In the old romance of Lancelot du Lac, the Demoiselle d'Escalot directed that after death her body should be placed richly adorned in a boat, and allowed to float away before the wind; a trace of the ancient belief in the passage over sea to the soul-land.

> There take the little bed on which I died
> For Lancelot's love, and deck it like the Queen's
> For richness, and me also like the Queen
> In all I have of rich, and lay me on it.
> And let there be prepared a chariot-bier
> To take me to the river, and a barge
> Be ready on the river, clothed in black.
>
> TENNYSON'S *Elaine*

And the grave-digger in Hamlet sings of being at death

> . . . shipp'd intill the land,
> As if I had never been such.
> Act v. Sc. I.

When King Arthur was about to die, with a mortal wound in the head, he was brought by good Sir Bedivere to the water's side.

'And when they were at the water's side, even fast by the banke, hoved a little barge with many faire ladies in it, and among them all was a queene, and all they had blacke hoods, and they wept and shriked when they saw King Arthur. "Now put mee into the barge," said the king; and so hee did softly; and there received him three queenes with great mourning, and so these three queenes set them downe, and in one of their laps King Arthur laide his head. And then that queene said, "Ah! deer brother, why have ye tarried so long from me? Alas! this wound on your head hath taken over much cold." And so then they rowed from the land, and Sir Bedivere cried, "Ah! my lord Arthur, what shall become of mee now ye goe from me, and leave me here alone among mine enemies?" "Comfort thy selfe," said King Arthur, "and do as well as thou maiest, for in mee is no trust for to trust in; for I wil into the vale of Avilion for to heale me of my greivous wound; and if thou never heere more of mee, pray for my soule." But evermore the queenes and the ladies wept and shriked that it was pity for to heare them. And as soone as Sir Bedivere had lost the sight of the barge, he wept and wailed, and so tooke the forrest.'

This fair Avalon –

> Where falls not hail, or rain, or any snow,
> Nor ever wind blows loudly; but – lies
> Deep-meadow'd, happy, fair with orchard lawns
> And bowery hollows crown'd with summer sea,

is the Isle of the Blessed of the Kelts. Tzetze and Procopius attempt to localize it, and suppose that the Land of Souls is Britain; but in this they are mistaken; as also are those who think to find Avalon at Glastonbury. Avalon is the Isle of Apples – a name reminding one of the Garden of the Hesperides in the far western seas, with its tree of golden apples in the midst. When we are told that in the remote Ogygia sleeps Kronos gently, watched by Briareus, till the time comes for his awaking, we have a Græcized form of the myth of Arthur in Avalon being cured of his grievous wound. It need hardly be said that the Arthur of romance is actually a demi-god, believed in long before the birth of the historic Arthur. This Ogygia, says Plutarch, lies due west, beneath the setting sun. According to an ancient poem published by M. Villemarqué, it is a place of enchanting beauty. There youths and maidens dance hand in hand on the dewy grass, green trees are laden with apples, and behind the woods the golden sun dips and rises. A murmuring rill flows from a spring in the midst of the island, and thence drink the spirits and obtain life with the draught. Joy, song, and minstrelsy reign in that blessed region. There all is plenty, and the golden age ever lasts; cows give their milk in such abundance that they fill large ponds at a milking. There, too, is a palace all of glass, floating in air, and receiving within its transparent walls the souls of the blessed: it is to this house of glass that Merddin Emrys and his nine bards voyage. To this alludes Taliesin in his poem, 'The Booty of the Deep', where he says, that the valour of Arthur is not retained in the glass enclosure. Into this mansion three classes of men obtain no admission – the tailors, of whom it takes nine to make a man, spending their days sitting, and whose hands, though they labour, are white; the warlocks, and the usurers.

In popular opinion, this distant isle was far more beautiful than paradise, and the rumours of its splendour so excited the mind of the mediaevals, that the western land became the subject of satyre and jest. It was nicknamed Cocaigne or Schlaraffenland.

An English poem, 'apparently written in the latter part of the thirteenth century', says Mr Wright (S. Patrick's Purgatory), 'which was printed very inaccurately by Hickes, from a manuscript which is now in the British Museum', describes Cocaigne as far away out to sea, west of Spain. Slightly modernized it runs thus: –

> Though Paradise be merry and bright,
> Cokaygne is of fairer sight;
> What is there in Paradise?
> Both grass and flower and green ris (boughs).
> Though there be joy and great dute (pleasure),
> There is not meat, but fruit.
> There is not hall, bower, nor bench,
> But water man's thirst to quench.

In Paradise are only two men, Enoch and Elias; but Cocaigne is full of happy men and women. There is no land like it under heaven; it is there always day and never night; there quarrelling and strife are unknown; there no people die; there falls neither hail, rain, or snow, neither is thunder heard there, nor blustering winds –

> There is a well fair abbaye
> Of white monks and of grey;
> There both bowers and halls,
> All of pasties be the walls,
> Of flesh, and fish, and rich meat,
> The like fullest that men may eat.
> Floweren cakes be the shingles all,
> Of church, cloister, bower, and hall.
> The pins be fat pudings,
> Rich meat to princes and kings.

The cloister is built of gems and spices, and all about are birds merrily singing, ready roasted flying into the hungry mouths; and there are buttered larks and 'garlek gret plenté'.

A French poem on this land describes it as a true cookery-land, as its nickname implies. All down the streets go roasted geese turning themselves; there is a river of wine; the ladies are all fair; every month one has new clothes. There bubbles up the fountain of perpetual youth, which will restore to bloom and vigour all who bathe in it, be they ever so old and ugly.

However much the burlesque poets of the Middle Ages might laugh at this mysterious western region of blissful souls, it held its own in the belief of the people.

Curiously enough, the same confusion between Britain and Avalon, which was made by Procopius, is still made by the German peasantry, who have their Engel-land which, through a similarity of name, they identify with England, to which they say, the souls of the dead are transported. In this land, according to Teutonic mythology, which in this point resembles the Keltic, is a glass mountain. In like manner the Slaves believe in a paradise for souls wherein is a large apple-orchard, in the midst of which rises a glass rock crowned with a golden palace; and in olden times they buried bear's claws with the dead, to assist him in climbing the crystal mountain.

The mysterious Western Land, in Irish, is called Thierna na oge, or the Country of Youth; and it is identified with a city of palaces and minsters sunk beneath the Atlantic, or at the bottom of lakes.

'The ancient Greek authors,' says M. de Latocnaye in his pleasant tour through Ireland, quoted by Crofton Croker, 'and Plato in particular, have recorded a tradition of an ancient world. They pretend that an immense island, or rather a vast continent, has been swallowed up by the sea to the west of Europe. It is more than probable that the inhabitants of Connemara have never heard of Plato or of the Greeks; nevertheless they have also their ancient tradition. "Our land will reappear some day," say the old men to the young folk, as they lead them on a certain day of the year to a mountain-top, and point out over the sea to them; the fishers also on their coasts pretend that they see towns and villages at the bottom of the water. The descriptions which they give of this imaginary country are as emphatic and exaggerated as those of the promised land: milk flows in some of the rivulets, others gush with wine; undoubtedly there are also streams of whisky and porter.'

The subject of cities beneath the water, which appear above the waves at dawn on Easter-day, or which can be seen by moonlight in the still depths of a lake, is too extensive to be considered here, opening up as it does questions of mythology which, to be fully discussed, would demand a separate paper. Each myth of antiquity touches other myths with either hand, and it is difficult to isolate one for consideration without being drawn into the discussion of other articles of belief on which it leans, and to which it is united. As in the sacred symbol of the Church each member predicates that which is to follow, and is a logical consequence of that which goes before, so that the excision of one article would destroy the completeness, and dissolve the unity of the faith – so, with the sacred beliefs of antiquity, one myth is linked to another, and cannot be detached without breaking into and destroying the harmony of the charmed circle.

But to confine ourselves to two points – the phantom western land, and the passage to it.

'Those who have read the history of the Canaries,' writes Washington Irving, 'may remember the wonders told of this enigmatical island. Occasionally it would be visible from their shores, stretching away in the clear bright west, to all appearance substantial like themselves, and still more beautiful. Expeditions would launch forth from the Canaries to explore this land of promise. For a time its sun-gilt peaks and long shadowy promontories would remain distinctly visible; but in proportion as the voyagers approached, peak and promontory would gradually fade away, until nothing would remain but blue sky above and deep blue water below.

'Hence this mysterious isle was stigmatized by ancient cosmographers with the name of Aprositus, or the inaccessible.' The natives of the Canaries relate to this island, which they name after S. Brandan, the following tale. In the early part of the fifteenth century, there arrived in Lisbon an old bewildered pilot of the seas, who had been driven by the tempests he knew not whither, and raved about an island in the far deep, upon which he had landed, and which he had found peopled with Christians and adorned with noble cities. The inhabitants told him they were descendants of a band of Christians who fled from Spain, when that country was conquered by the Moslems. They were curious about the state of their fatherland, and grieved to hear that the Moslem still held possession of the kingdom of Granada. The old man, on his return to his ship, was caught by a tempest, whirled out once more to sea, and saw no more of the unknown island. This strange story caused no little excitement in Portugal and Spain. Those well versed in history remembered to have read that in the time of the conquest of Spain, in the eighth century, seven bishops, at the head of seven bands of exiles, had fled across the great ocean to some distant shores, where they might found seven Christian cities, and enjoy their faith unmolested. The fate of these wanderers had hitherto remained a mystery, and their story had faded from memory; but the report of the old pilot revived the long-forgotten theme, and it was determined, by the pious and enthusiastic, that this island thus accidentally discovered was the identical place of refuge, whither the wandering bishops had been guided with their flock by the hand of Providence. No one, however, entered into the matter with half the zeal of Don Fernando de Alma, a young cavalier of high standing in the Portuguese court, and of the meek, sanguine, and romantic temperament. The Island of the Seven Cities became now the constant subject of his thoughts by day and of his dreams by night; and he determined to fit out an expedition, and set sail in quest of the sainted island. Don Ioacos II furnished him with a commission, constituting him Adalantado, or governor, of any country he might discover, with the single proviso, that he should bear all the expenses of the discovery, and pay a tenth of the profits to the crown. With two vessels he put out to sea and steered for the Canaries – in those days the regions of nautical discovery and romance, and the outposts of the known world; for as yet Columbus had not crossed the ocean. Scarce had they reached those latitudes, than they were separated by a violent tempest. For many days the caravel of Don Fernando was driven about at the mercy of the elements, and the crew were in despair. All at once the storm subsided, the ocean sank into a calm, the clouds which had veiled the face of heaven were suddenly withdrawn, and the tempest-tossed mariners beheld a fair and mountainous island, emerging, as if by enchantment, from the murky gloom. The caravel now lay perfectly becalmed off the mouth of a river, on the banks of which, about a league off, was described a noble city, with lofty walls and towers, and a protecting castle. After a time, a stately barge with sixteen oars was seen emerging from the river and approaching the vessel. Under a silken canopy in the stern sat a richly-clad cavalier, and over his head was a banner bearing the sacred emblem of the cross. When the barge reached the caravel, the cavalier stepped on board and, in the old Castilian language, welcomed the strangers to the Island of the Seven Cities. Don Fernando could scarce believe that this was not all a dream. He made known his name and the object of his voyage. The Grand Chamberlain – such was the title of the cavalier from the island – assured him that, as soon as his credentials were presented, he would be acknowledged as the Adalantado of the Seven Cities. In the mean time, the day was waning; the barge was ready to convey him to land, and would assuredly bring him back. Don Fernando leaped into it after the Grand Chamberlain, and was rowed ashore. Every thing there bore the stamp of former ages, as if the world had suddenly rolled back for several centuries; and no wonder, for the Island of the Seven Cities had been cut off from the rest of the world for several hundred years. On shore Don Fernando spent an agreeable evening at the court-house, and late at night with reluctance he re-entered the barge, to return to his vessel. The barge sallied out to sea, but no caravel was to be seen. The oarsmen rowed on – their monotonous chant had a lulling effect. A drowsy influence crept over Don Fernando: objects swam before his eyes, and he lost consciousness. On his recovery, he found himself in a strange cabin, surrounded by strangers. Where was he? On board a Portuguese ship, bound for Lisbon. How had he come there? He had been taken senseless from a wreck drifting about the ocean. The vessel arrived in the Tagus, and anchored before the famous capital. Don Fernando sprang joyfully on shore, and hastened to his ancestral mansion. A strange porter opened the door, who knew nothing of him or of his family: no people of the name had inhabited the house for many a year. He sought the house of his betrothed, the Donna Serafina. He beheld her on the balcony; then he raised his arms towards her with an exclamation of rapture. She cast upon him a look of indignation, and hastily retired. He rang at the door; as it was opened by the porter he rushed past, sought the well-known chamber, and threw himself at the feet of Serafina. She started back with affright, and took refuge in the arms of a youthful cavalier.

'What mean you, Señor?' cried the latter.

'What right have you to ask that question?' demanded Don Fernando fiecely.

'The right of an affianced suitor!'

'O Serafina! is this your fidelity?' cried he in a tone of agony.

'Serafina! What mean you by Serafina, Señor? This lady's name is Maria.'

'What!' cried Don Fernando; 'is not this Serafina Alvarez, the original of yon portrait which smiles on me from the wall?'

'Holy Virgin!' cried the young lady, casting her eyes upon the portrait, 'he is talking of my great-grandmother!'

With this Portuguese legend, which has been charmingly told by Washington Irving, must be compared the adventures of Porsenna, king of Russia, in the sixth volume of Dodsley's 'Poetical Collection'. Porsenna was carried off by Zephyr to a distant region, where the scenery was enchanting, the flowers ever in bloom, and creation put on her fairest guise. There he found a princess with whom he spent a few agreeable weeks. Being, however, anxious to return to his kingdom, he took leave of her, saying that after three months' absence his return would be necessary.

> 'Three months!' replied the fair, 'three months alone!
> Know that three hundred years are roll'd away
> Since at my feet my lovely Phœnix lay.'
> 'Three hundred years!' re-echoed back the prince:
> 'A whole three hundred years completed since
> I landed here?'

On his return to Russia, he was overtaken by all-conquering time, and died. A precisely similar legend exists in Ireland.

In a similar manner Ogier-le-Danois found himself unconscious of the lapse of time in Avalon. He was one day carried by his steed Papillon along a track of light to the mystic Vale of Apples; there he alighted beside a sparkling fountain, around which waved bushes of fragrant flowering shrubs. By the fountain stood a beautiful maiden, extending to him a golden crown wreathed with blossoms. He put it on his head, and at once forgot the past: his battles, his love of glory, Charlemagne and his preux, died from his memory like a dream. He saw only Morgana, and felt no desire other than to sigh through eternity at her feet. One day the crown slipped from Ogier's head, and fell into the fountain: immediately his memory returned, and the thoughts of his friends and relatives, and military prowess, troubled his peace of mind. He begged Morgana to permit him to return to earth. She consented, and he found that, in the few hours of rapture in Avalon, two hundred years had elapsed. Charlemagne, Roland, and Oliver were no more. Hugh Capet sat on the throne of France, the dynasty of the great Charles having come to an end. Ogier found no rest in France, and he returned to Avalon, nevermore to leave the fay Morgana.

In the Portuguese legend, the Island of the Seven Cities is unquestionably the land of departed spirits of the ancient Celtiberians; the properties of the old belief remain: the barge to conduct the spirit to the shore, the gorgeous scenery, and the splendid castle, but the significance of the myth has been lost, and a story of a Spanish colony having taken refuge in the far western sea has been invented, to account for the Don meeting with those of his own race in the phantom isle.

That the belief in this region was very strong in Ireland, about the eleventh century, is certain from its adoption into the popular mythology of the Norsemen, under the name of Greater Ireland (Ireland hit Mikla). Till the ruin of the Norse kingdom in the east of Erin, in the great battle of Clontarf (1114), the Norsemen were brought much in contact with the Irish, and by this means adopted Irish names, such as Nial and Cormac, and Irish superstitions as well. The name they gave to the Isle of the Blessed, in the western seas, was either Great Ireland, because there the Erse tongue was spoken, – it being a colony of the souls of the Kelts, – or Hvitramannaland, because there the inhabitants were robed in white. In the mediaeval vision of Owayne the Knight, which is simply a fragment of Keltic mythology in a Christian garb, the paradise is enclosed by a fair wall, 'whyte and brygth as glass', a reminiscence of the glass-palace in Avalon, and the inhabitants of that land –

Fayre vestymentes they hadde on.

Some of these met him on his first starting on his journey, and there were fifteen in long white garments.

The following passages in the Icelandic chronicles refer to this land of mystery and romance.

'Mar of Holum married Thorkatla, and their son was Ari; he was storm-cast on the White-man's land, which some call Great Ireland; this lies in the Western Sea near Vinland the Good (America): it is called six days' sail due west from Ireland. Ari could never leave it, and there he was baptized. Hrafn, who sailed to Limerick, was the first to tell of this; he had spent a long time in Limerick in Ireland.'

This passage is from the Landnámabok, a work of the twelfth century. A turbulent Icelander, named Bjorn of Bradwick, vanished from his home. Years after, a native of the same island, Gudlief by name, was trading between Iceland and Dublin, when, somewhere about the year 1000, he was caught by a furious gale from the east, and driven further in the western seas than he had ever visited before. Here he came upon a land well populated, where the people spoke the Irish tongue. The crew were taken before an assembly of the natives, and would probably have been hardly dealt with, had not a tall man ridden up, surrounded by an armed band, to whom all bowed the knee. This man spoke to Gudlief in the Norse tongue, and asked him whence he came. On hearing that he was an Icelander, he made particular inquiries about the residents in the immediate neighbourhood of Bradwick, and gave Gudlief a ring and a sword, to be taken to friends at home. Then he bade him return at once to Iceland, and warn his kindred not to seek him in his new home. Gudlief put again to sea, and, arriving safely in Iceland, related his adventures, concluding that the man he had seen was Bjorn of Bradwick. Another Icelander brought away two children from Vinland, and they related that near their home was a land, where people walked about in flowing white robes, singing processional psalms. Northern antiquarians attempt to identify this White-man's land with Florida, where they suppose was settled the Welsh colony led beyond the sea by Madoc in 1169. I have little doubt that it is simply an Icelandic reminiscence of the popular Irish superstition relative to the Soul Island beneath the setting sun.

> In his crystal ark,
> Whither sail'd Merlin was his band of bards,
> Old Merlin, master of the mystic lore;
> Belike his crystal ark, instinct with life,
> Obedient to the mighty Master, reach'd
> The Land of the Departed; there, belike,
> They in the clime of immortality,
> Themselves immortal, drink the gales of bliss
> Which o'er Flathinnis breathe eternal spring,
> Blending whatever odours make the gale
> Of evening sweet, whatever melody
> Charms the wood traveller.
>
> SOUTHEY'S *Madoc*, xi.

This Flath Innis, the Noble Island, is the Gaelic name for the western paradise. Macpherson, in his Introduction to the "History of Great Britain", relates a legend which agrees with those prevalent among other Keltic peoples. In former days there lived in Skerr a Druid of renown. He sat with his face to the west on the shore, his eye following the declining sun, and he blamed the careless billows which tumbled between him and the distant Isle of Green. One day, as he sat musing on a rock, a storm arose on the sea; a cloud, under whose squally skirts the foaming waters tossed, rushed suddenly into the bay, and from its dark womb emerged a boat with white sails bent to the wind, and banks of gleaming oars on either side. But it was destitute of mariners, itself seeming to live and move. An unusual terror seized on the aged Druid; he heard a voice call, 'Arise, and see the Green Isle of those who have passed away!' Then he entered the vessel. Immediately the wind shifted, the cloud enveloped him, and in the bosom of the vapour he sailed away. Seven days gleamed on him through the mist; on the eighth, the waves rolled violently, the vessel pitched, and darkness thickened around him, when suddenly he heard a cry, 'The Isle! the Isle!' The clouds parted before him, the waves abated, the wind died away, and the vessel rushed into dazzling light. Before his eyes lay the Isle of the Departed basking in golden light. Its hills sloped green and tufted with beauteous trees to the shore, the mountain-tops were enveloped in bright and transparent clouds, from which gushed limpid streams, which, wandering down the steep hill-sides with pleasant harp-like murmur, emptied themselves into the twinkling blue bays. The valleys were open and free to the ocean; trees loaded with leaves, which scarcely waved to the light breeze, were scattered on the green declivities and rising ground; all was calm and bright; the pure sun of autumn shone from his blue sky on the fields; he hastened not to the west for repose, nor was he seen to rise in the east, but hung as a golden lamp, ever illumining the Fortunate Isle.

There, in radiant halls, dwelt the spirits of the departed, ever blooming and beautiful, ever laughing and gay.

It is curious to note how retentive of ancient mythologic doctrines relative to death are the memories of the people. This Keltic fable of the 'Land beyond the Sea', to which the souls are borne after death, has engrafted itself on popular religion in England. The following hymn is from the collection of the Sunday School Union, and is founded on this venerable Druidic tenet: –

Shall we meet beyond the river,
    Where the surges cease to roll,
Where in all the bright For-ever
    Sorrow ne'er shall press the soul?

Shall we meet in that blest harbour,
    When our stormy voyage is o'er?
Shall we meet and cast the anchor
    By the fair celestial shore?

Shall we meet with many loved ones,
    Who were torn from our embrace?
Shall we listen to their voices,
    And behold them face to face?

So is a hymn from the Countess of Huntingdon's collection: –

I launch into the deep,
And leave my native land,
Where sin lulls all asleep:
For thee I fain would all resign,
And sail for heav'n with thee and thine.

Come, heav'nly wind, and blow
A prosp'rous gale of grace,
To waft from all below
To heav'n, my destined place:
There in full sail my port I'll find,
And leave the world and sin behind.

Or I might quote a poem on 'The Last Voyage', from the Lyra Messianica, which one would have supposed to have been founded on the Gaelic legend told by Macpherson: –

On! on! through the storm and the billow,
  By life's chequer'd troubles opprest,
The rude deck my home and my pillow,
  I sail to the land of the Blest.

The tempests of darkness confound me,
  Above me the deep waters roll,
But the arms of sweet Pity surround me,
  And bear up my foundering soul.

With a wild and mysterious commotion
  The torrent flows, rapid and strong;
Towards a mournful and shadowy ocean
  My vessel bounds fiercely along.
Ye waters of gloom and of sorrow,
  How dread are your tumult and roar!
But, on! for the brilliant to-morrow
  That dawns upon yonder bright shore!

O Pilot, the great and the glorious,
  That sittest in garments so white,
O'er death and o'er hell 'The Victorious',
  The Way and the Truth and the Light,
Speak, speak to the darkness appalling,
  And bid the mad turmoil to cease:
For, hark! the good Angels are calling
  My soul to the haven of Peace.

Now, ended all singing and sadness,
  The waves of destruction all spent,
I sing with the children of gladness
  The song of immortal content.

It would be a study of no ordinary interest to trace modern popular Protestantism back to the mythologic systems of which it is the resultant. The early Fathers erred in regarding the ancient heresies as bastard forms of Christianity; they were distinct religions, feebly tinged by contact with the religion of the Cross. In like manner, I am satisfied that we make a mistake in considering the Dissent of England, especially as manifested in greatest intensity in the wilds of Cornwall, Wales, and the eastern moors of Yorkshire, where the Keltic element is strong, as a form of Christianity. It is radically different: its framework and nerve is of ancient British origin, passing itself off as a spiritual Christianity.

In S. Peter's, Rome, is a statue of Jupiter, deprived of his thunderbolt, which is replaced by the emblematic keys. In like manner, much of the religion of the lower orders, which we regard as essentially Christian, is ancient heathenism, refitted with Christian symbols. The story of Jacob's stratagem is reversed: the voice is the elder brother's voice, but the hands and the raiment are those of the younger.

I have instanced the belief in angelic music calling away the soul as one heathen item in popular Protestant mythology –

> Hark! they whisper! Angels say,
> 'Sister spirit, come away!'

Another is embodied in the tenet that the souls of the departed become angels. In Judaic and Christian doctrine, the angel creation is distinct from that of human beings, and a Jew or a Catholic would as little dream of confusing the distinct conception of angel and soul, as of believing in metempsychosis. But not so dissenting religion. According to Druidic dogma, the souls of the dead were guardians of the living; a belief shared with the ancient Indians, who venerated the spirits of their ancestry, the Pitris, as watching over and protecting them. Thus, the hymn 'I want to be an Angel', so popular in dissenting schools, is founded on the venerable Aryan myth, and therefore of exceeding interest; but Christian it is not.

Another tenet which militates against Christian doctrine, and has supplanted it in popular belief, is that of the transmigration of the soul to bliss immediately on its departure from the body.

The article *stantis vel cadentis Fidei*, of the Apostles, was the resurrection of the body. If we read the Acts of the Apostles and their Epistles with care, it is striking how great weight, we find, is laid on this doctrine. They went every where preaching – 1. the rising of Christ; 2. the consequent restoration of the bodies of Christians. 'If the dead rise not, then is not Christ raised; and if Christ be not raised, your faith is vain. But now is Christ risen from the dead, and become the first fruits of them that slept. For as in Adam all die, even so in Christ shall all be made alive.' This was the key-note to the teaching of the Apostles; it runs through the New Testament, and is reflected in the writings of the Fathers. It occupies its legitimate position in the Creeds, and the Church has never failed to insist upon it with no faltering voice.

But the doctrine of the soul being transported to heaven, and of its happiness being completed at death, finds no place in the Bible or the Liturgies of any branch – Greek, Roman, or Anglican – of the Church Catholic. Yet this was the tenet of our Keltic forefathers, and it has maintained itself in English Protestantism, so as to divest the doctrine of the resurrection of the body of its grasp on the popular mind. Among the Kelts, again, reception into the sacred inner circle of the illuminated was precisely analogous to the received dissenting doctrine of conversion. To it are applied, by the bards, terms such as 'the second birth', 'the renewal', which are to this day employed by Methodists to designate the mysterious process of conversion.

But to return to the subject of this article. It is a singular fact, that only the other day I heard of a man in Cleveland, being buried two years ago with a candle, a penny, and a bottle of wine in his coffin: the candle to light him along the road, the penny to pay the ferry, and the wine to nourish him, as he went to the New Jerusalem. I was told this, and this explanation was given me, by some rustics who professed to have attended the funeral. This looks to me as though the shipping into the other land were not regarded merely as a figure of speech, but as a reality.

CHAPTER 10

Swan-Maidens

NYONE WHO has watched swans landing or taking off from a sheet of still water, or simply flying overhead in graceful skeins, cannot help but understand why these birds have been so often associated with magic or mystery. In the *Dictionary of Mythology, Folklore and Symbolism* by Gertrude Jobes, the following 'symbolic meanings' are listed for the swan: beauty, cloud, death, dignity, eternity, excellence, faithfulness, grace, haughtiness, mist, music, perfect discernment, poetry, prophecy, purity, snow, solitude, summer, wind, wisdom and, most importantly, the ability to discern essential things from non-essential (this because swans are widely believed to separate milk from water when the two are mixed). Additional meanings are swans as vehicles for the soul's journey and, thus, resurrection.

Swans are sacred to Aphrodite, who in classical myth rides in a chariot drawn by swans, to Apollo, Brahma Jupiter, Leda, Orpheus, Sarasvati, Venus and Zeus, as well as to the Christian saints Cuthbert and Hugh of Lincoln. In the Arthurian story of Guingamore and Gueherres a mysterious ship, drawn by a swan, appears at the castle where King Arthur is sleeping. He is awakened by a storm and sees the boat which, on investigation, proves to carry the body of a slain knight who is later avenged in this most mysterious of stories. Once the body is taken from the boat the swan departs, drawing the craft by means of silver chains attached to a jewelled collar.

Swans were of great symbolic importance to the ancient classical world, despite the fact that they were quite rare in the Mediterranean, and it is interesting that Homer praises the singing swan which, unlike the mute swan, lives only in the Northern hemisphere. Stories of the song emitted by the swan as it was about to die seem to have travelled widely, and may well have given rise to the idea both of the swan's prophetic abilities and even to the Swan-Maiden stories themselves.

This northern focus may also, curiously enough, account for the association of swans with the Greek god Apollo, who was given great reverence by the northern tribe of Hyperboreans, believed to live 'somewhere at the back of the North wind' or sometimes in a mysterious land which has been identified with Britain. There Apollo used to come every twenty-two years to be worshipped in a great golden circular temple of stones which has been identified by some with Stonehenge.

The song emitted by the dying bird (which has given us the term 'swan-song', referring to the final work of any great artist) also led to the association of the swan with Christ, whose seven last words from the Cross were associated with the last notes of the swan's death-cry.

Curiously enough, despite the generally positive nature of the symbolic references to the swan, in certain medieval bestiaries a strangely negative interpretation appears. This is due to the contrast between the snowy plumage of the bird and its dark flesh, which is termed 'black' by some interpreters and is thus seen to represent the hypocrite 'whose black sinful flesh is clothed in white garments'.

The swan is an important symbol in heraldry and frequently appears in the coats of arms of cities such as Zwickau in Bavaria, the original name of which was Cygnea, the city of the Swan. A chivalric Order of the Swan was founded in 1440 and renewed in 1843 by the German king Freidrich Wilhelm IV as a charitable foundation, though apparently it never functioned, but fell into desuetude with the advent of the First World War.

In Asia Minor, Scandinavia and the Slavic lands, as well as in India, China, Japan and Arabia, the symbolism of the swan is almost entirely focused on the feminine aspect, and it is from these lands in particular that the stories of Swan-Maidens come. In classical antiquity equal importance was given to the male swan, as in the story of Zeus and Leda, while it appears to have been male birds which drew the chariots of Apollo and were recognized as symbolic of god-like virility.

Among the Celtic peoples, swans were ever associated with the Otherworld and several of the most powerful stories of the Swan-Maidens originate in Ireland. As well as the 'Children of Lir' story mentioned by Gould, there is also that of Caer Ibormeith, a beautiful woman of the *sidhe* who frequently took the form of a swan and whom the love-god Aengus mac ind Oic dreamed of and subsequently sought out. In another tale the Ulster hero Chuchulainn harnesses a flock of swans to his chariot when it becomes stuck in the mud; and later in the cycle of stories which constellated around this figure, he is pursued by a woman named Derbforgail, who follows him, along with her maidservant, in the form of two swans. Cuchulainn takes a shot at the birds with his sling and strikes Derbforgail to the ground, where she regains her human form. Sorry for what he has done, Cuchulainn sucks out the stone which had lodged in her shoulder but in so doing tastes her blood and is thus forbidden by an ancient taboo to mate with her.

In nearly all of the instances quoted here, and in the chapter which follows, this

113

theme is once again a reflection of the mutual desire of humans and faery people to marry into the opposite stock.

*　　*　　*

I REMEMBER a long scramble in Iceland, over the ruins of tuff rock in a narrow gorge. My little pony had toiled sturdily up a dusty slope leading apparently to nothing, when, all at once, the ravine terminated in an abrupt scarp, whence was obtained a sudden peep of entrancing beauty. Far away in front gleamed a snowy dome of silver, doubly refined and burnished, resting upon a basement of gentian blue.

> Some blue peaks in the distance rose,
> And white against the cold-white sky
> Shone out their crowning snows.

To the left started sheer precipices of ink-black rock to icy pinnacles, from which fell a continuous powder of white water into a lake, here black as the rocks above it, yonder bluer than the over-arching heavens. Not a sound of animated life broke the stillness, which would have been oppressive, but for the patter of the falling streams. The only living objects visible were two white swans rippling proudly through the clear water.

I have never since felt surprise at superstition attaching itself to these glorious birds, haunting lone tarns, pure as new-fallen snow. The first night I slept under my tent in the same island, I was wakened with a start by a wild triumphant strain as of clarions pealing from the sky. I crept from under canvas to look up, and saw a flight of the Hooper swans on their way to the lakes of the interior, high up, lit by the sun, like flakes of gold-leaf against the green sky of an arctic night.

Its solitary habits, the purity of its feathers, its wondrous song, have given to the wild swan a charm which has endeared it to poets, and ensured its introduction into mythology.

The ancient Indians, looking up at the sky over which coursed the white cirrus clouds, fabled of a heavenly lake in which bathed the swan-like Apsaras, impersonifications of these delicate light cloud-flakes. What these white vapours were, the ancient Aryans could not understand; therefore, because they bore a more or less remote resemblance to swans floating on blue waters, they supposed them to be divine beings partaking of the nature and appearance of these beautiful birds.

The name Apsaras signifies those who go in the water, from *ap*, water, and *saras*, from sr, to go. Those who bear the name skim as swans over the lotus-pond of heaven, or, laying aside their feather-dresses, bathe, as beautiful females, in the limpid flood. These swan-maidens are the houris of the Vedic heaven; receiving to their arms the souls of the heroes. Sometimes they descend to earth, and become the wives of mortals; but soon their celestial nature re-asserts itself, and they expand their luminous wings, and soar away into the heavenly deeps of tranquil azure. I have elsewhere referred to the story of Urvaçi, the Apsaras, and her lover Puravaras. And Somadeva relates the adventures of a certain Niçcayadatta, who caught one of these celestial maidens, and then lost her, but, full of love, pursued her to the golden city above. He tells also of Srîdatta, who beheld one bathing in the Ganges, and, plunging after her, found himself in a wondrous land beneath the water, in the company of the beloved.

In the Kalmuk collection of tales called Siddhi-Kûr, which is a translation from the Sanskrit, is a story of a woman who had three daughters. The girls took it in turn to keep the cattle. An ox was lost, and the eldest, in search of it, entered a cave, where she found an extensive lake of rippling blue water, on which swam a stainless swan. She asked for her ox, and the bird replied that she should have it if she would become his wife. She refused and returned to her mother. Next day the second sister lost an ox, traced it to the cave, pursued it into the land of mysteries, and saw the blue lake surrounded by flowery banks, on which floated a silver swan. She refused to become his wife, as did her sister. Next day the same incidents were repeated with the third sister, who, however, proved more compliant to the wishes of the swan.

The Samojeds have a wild tale about swan-maidens. Two Samojeds lived in a desolate moor, where they caught foxes, sables, and bears. One went on a journey, the other remained at home. He who travelled, reached an old woman chopping birch-trees. He cut down the trees for her, and drew them to her tent. This gratified the old woman, and she bade him hide, and see what would take place. He concealed himself; and shortly after beheld seven maidens approach. They asked the old woman whether she had cut the wood herself, and then whether she was quite alone. To both questions she replied in the affirmative; then they went away. The old woman then drew the Samojed from his hiding-place, and bade him follow the traces of the damsels, and steal the dress of one of them. He obeyed. Emerging from a wood of gloomy pines, he came upon a beautiful lake, in which swam the seven maidens. Then the man took away the dress which lay nearest to him. The seven swam to the shore and sought their clothes. Those of one were gone. She cried bitterly, and exclaimed, 'I will be the wife of him who has stolen my dress, if he will restore it me.' He replied, 'No, I will not give you back your feather dress, or you will spread your wings, and fly away from me.'

'Give me my clothes, I am freezing!'

'Not far from here are seven Samojeds, who range the neighbourhood by day, and at night hang their hearts on the tent-pegs. Procure for me these hearts, and I will give you the clothes.'

'In five days I will bring them to you.'

Then he gave her the clothes, and returned to his companion.

One day the maiden came to him out of the sky, and asked him to accompany her to the brothers, whose hearts he had set her to procure. They came to the tent, and the man secreted himself, but the damsel became invisible. At night the seven Samojeds returned, ate their supper, and then hitched up their hearts to the tent-pegs. The swan-maiden stole them, and brought them to her lover. He dashed all but one upon the ground, and as they fell, the brothers expired. Then the man without a heart awoke, and entreated to have it returned to him.

'Once upon a time you killed my mother,' said the Samojed; 'restore her to life, and you shall have your heart.'

Then the man without the heart said to his wife, 'Go to the place where the dead lie, there you will find a purse, in that purse is her soul; shake the purse over the dead woman's bones, and she will come to life.' The woman did as she was ordered, and the mother of the Samojed revived. Then he dashed the heart to the ground, and the last of the seven brothers died.

But the swan-maiden took her own heart and that of her husband, and threw them into the air. The mother of the Samojed saw that they were without hearts, so she went to the lake where swam the six maidens; she stole one dress, and would not restore it till the maiden had promised to recover the hearts which were in the air. This she succeeded in doing, and her dress was restored.

Among the Minussinian Tatars these mysterious ladies have lost their grace and beauty. They dwell in the seventeenth region of the earth in raven-black rocks, and are fierce, raging demons of the air. They scourge themselves into action with a sword, lap the blood of the slain, and fly gorged with blood for forty years. In number they are forty, and yet they run together into one; so that at one time there is but a single swan-woman, at another the sky is dark with their numerous wings; a description which makes it easy to identify them with clouds. But there are not only evil swan-women, there are also good ones as well.

Katai Khan lived on the coast of the White Sea, at the foot of gloomy mountains. He had two daughters, Kara Kuruptju (black thimble) and Kesel Djibäk (red silk); the elder evil disposed and in league with the powers of darkness, a friend of the raging swan-woman; the younger beautiful and good.

> Kesel Djibäk often riseth,
> In a dress of snowy swan,
> To the realm where reign the Kudai.
> There the Kudai's daughters seven
> Fly on wings of snowy swan;
> With them sporteth Kessel Djibäk,
> Swimming on the golden lake.

The seven Kudai, or gods of the Tatars, are the planets. Kara Kuruptju is the evening twilight, Kessel Djibäk the morning dawn which ascends to the heavens, and there lingers among the floating feathery clouds. But Kara Kuruptju descends to the gloomy realm of the evil-hearted swan-women, where she marries their son Djidar Mos (bronzen), the thunder-cloud. These grimly swanlike damsels of the Tatars irresistibly remind us of the Phorcydæ; κυκνόμορφοι, as Æschylus calls them.

The classic swan myths must be considered in greater detail. They are numerous, for each Greek tribe had its own favourite myths, and additional fables were being constantly imported into religion from foreign sources. The swan was with the Greeks the bird of the Muses, and therefore also of Apollo. When the golden-haired deity was born, swans came from the golden stream of Pactolus, and seven times wheeled about Delos, uttering songs of joy.

> Seven times, on snowy pinions, circle round
> The Delian shores, and skim along the ground:
> The vocal birds, the favourites of the Nine,
> In strains melodious hail the birth divine.
> Oft as they carol on resounding wings,
> To soothe Latona's pangs, as many strings
> Apollo fitted to the warbling lyre
> In aftertimes; but ere the sacred choir
> Of circling swans another concert sung,
> In melting notes, the power immortal sprung
> To glorious birth.

A picture, this, of the white cloudlets fleeting around the rising sun.

The Muses were originally nymphs, and are the representatives of the Indian Apsaras; and it is on this account that the swans are their symbols. Beyond the Eridanus, in the land of the Lygii (Λίγυες, i.e. the clear-ringing), lived once a songful (μουσικός) king. Him Apollo transformed into a swan. 'Cycnus having left his kingdom, accompanied by his sisters, was filling the verdant banks, and the river Eridanus, and the forest, with his complaints; when the human voice becomes shrill, and grey feathers conceal his hair. A long neck, too, extends from his breast, and a membrane joins his reddening toes; plumage clothes his sides, and his mouth becomes a pointless bill. Cycnus becomes a new bird; but he trusts himself neither to heavens nor the air. He frequents the pools and wide meers, and abhorring fires, chooses the streams.' This Cycnus was a son of Sthenelus; he is the same as the son of Pelopea by Ares, and the son of Thyria by Poseidon. The son of Ares lived in southern Thessaly, where he slew pilgrims till Apollo cut off his head, and gave the skull to the temple of Ares. According to another version of the story, he was the son of Ares by Pyrene. When Herakles had slain him, the father was so enraged that he fought with the hero of many labours.

Cycnus, a son of Poseidon, was matched against Achilles, who, stripping him of his armour, suddenly beheld him transformed into a swan; or he is the son of Hyrie, who springs from a rock and becomes the bird from which he derives his name, whilst his mother dissolving into tears is transformed into a lake whereon the stately bird can glide.

In the fable of Leda, Zeus, the heaven above, clothed in swan's shape, – that is, enveloped in white mist, – embraces the fair Leda, who is probably the earth-mother, and by her becomes the father of the Dioscuri, the morning and evening twilights, and, according to some, of beautiful Helen, that is, Selene, the moon. The husband of Leda was Tyndareos, a name which identifies him with the thunderer, and he is therefore the same as Zeus.

According to the Cyprian legend, Nemesis, flying the pursuit of Zeus, took the form of a swan, and dropped an egg, from which issued Helen. Nemesis is a Norn, who, with Shame, 'having abandoned men, depart, *when they have clad their fair skin in white raiment*, to the tribe of the immortals.'

Swans were kept and fed as sacred birds on the Eurotas, and were reverenced in Sparta as emblems of Aphrodite: this is not surprising, as Aphrodite is identical with Helen, the moon, which swims at night as a silver swan upon the deep dark sky-sea. A late fable relates how that Achilles and Helen were united on a spirit-isle in Northern Pontus, where they were served by flights of white birds.

In the North, however, is the home of the swan, and there we find the fables about the mystic bird in great profusion. There, as a Faroese ballad says –

> Fly along, o'er the verdant ground,
> Glimmering swans to the rippling sound;

or, as an Icelandic song has it –

> Sweetly swans are singing
> In the summer time.
> There a swan as silver white,

118

In the summer time,
Lay upon my bosom light.
Lily maiden,
Sweetly swans are singing!

The venerable Edda of Soemund relates how that there were once three brothers, sons of a king of the Finns; one was called Slagfid, the second Egil, the third Völund, the original of our Wayland smith. They went on snow-shoes and hunted wild beasts. They came to Ulfdal, and there made themselves a house, where there is a water called the Wolflake. Early one morning they found, on the border of the lake, three maidens sitting and spinning flax. Near them lay their swan plumages: they were Valkyries. Two of them, Hladgud, the Swan-white, and Hervör, the All-white, were daughters of King Hlödver; the third was Olrun, a daughter of Kiàr of Valland. They took them home with them to their dwelling: Egil had Olrun, Slagfid had Swan-white, and Völund All-white. They lived there seven years, and then they flew away, seeking conflicts, and did not return. Egil then went on snow-shoes in search of Olrun, and Slagfid in search of Swan-white, but Völund remained in Wolfdale. In the German story of the mighty smith, as preserved in the Wilkina Saga, this incident has disappeared; but that the myth was Teutonic as well as Scandinavian, appears from the poem on Frederick of Suabia, a composition of the fourteenth century, wherein is related how the hero wanders in search of his beloved Angelburga. By chance he arrives at a fountain, in which are bathing three maidens, with their dresses, consisting of doves' feathers, lying at the side. Wieland, armed with a root which renders him invisible, approaches the bank and steals the clothes. The maidens, on discovering their loss, utter cries of distress. Wieland appears, and promises to return their bird-skins if one of them will consent to be his wife. They agree to the terms, leaving the choice to Wieland, who selects Angelburga, whom he had long loved without having seen. Brunhild, who was won by Sigurd, and who died for him, is said to 'move on her seat as a swan rocking on a wave', and the three sea-maids from whom Hagne stole a dress, which is simply described as 'wonderful' in the Nibelungen-Lied, are said to –

swim as birds before him on the flood.

An old German story tells of a nobleman who was hunting in a forest, when he emerged upon a lake in which bathed an exquisitely beautiful maiden. He stole up to her, and took from her the gold necklace she wore; then she lost her power to fly, and she became his wife. At one birth she bore seven sons, who had all of them gold chains round their necks, and had the power, which their mother had possessed, of transforming themselves into swans at pleasure. In the ancient Gudrun-Lied, an angel approaches like a swimming wild-bird.

A Hessian forester once saw a beautiful swan floating on a lonely lake. Charmed with its beauty, he prepared to shoot it, when it exclaimed, 'Shoot not, or it will cost you your life!' As he persisted in taking aim, the swan was suddenly transformed into a lovely girl, who swam towards him, and told him that she was bewitched, but could be freed if he would say an 'Our Father' every Sunday for her during a twelve-month, and not allude to what he had seen in conversation with his friends. He promised, but failed to keep silence, and lost her.

A hunter in Southern Germany lost his wife, and was in deep affliction. He went to a hermit and asked his advice; the aged man advised him to seek a lonely pool, and wait there till he saw three swans alight and despoil themselves of their feathers, then he was to steal one of the dresses, and never return it, but take the maiden whose was the vesture of plumes to be his wife. This the huntsman did, and he lived happily with the beautiful damsel for fifteen years. But one day he forgot to lock the cupboard in which he kept the feather-dress; the wife discovered it, put it on, spread her wings, and never returned. In some household tales a wicked step-mother throws white skirts over her step-children, and they are at once transformed into swans. A similar story is that of Hasan of Basra in the Arabian Nights.

The old fables of Valkyries were misunderstood when Christianity had cast these damsels from heaven, and the stories were modified to account for the transformation. The sweet maidens no more swam of their own free will in the crystal waves, but swam thus through the force of an enchantment they were unable to break. Thus, in the Irish legend of Fionmala, the daughter of King Lir, on the death of the mother of Fingula (Fionmala) and her brothers, their father married the wicked Aoife, who, through spite, transforms the children of Lir into swans, which must float on the waters for centuries, till the first mass-bell tingles. Who does not remember Tom Moore's verses on this legend? –

> Silent, O Moyle, be the roar of thy water;
>   Break not, ye breezes, your chain of repose,
> While, murmuring mournfully, Lir's lovely daughter
>   Tells to the night-star the tale of her woes.
> When shall the swan, her death-note singing,
>   Sleep with wings in darkness furl'd?
> When will heaven, its sweet bells ringing,
>   Call my spirit from this stormy world?
>
> Sadly, O Moyle, to thy winter-wave weeping,
>   Fate bids me languish long ages away;
> Yet still in her darkness doth Erin lie sleeping,
>   Still doth the pure light its dawning delay.
> When will that day-star, mildly springing,
>   Warm our isle with peace and love?
> When will heaven, its sweet bells ringing,
>   Call my spirit to the fields above?

In another version of the story there is no term fixed for the breaking of the enchantment; but when the bells of Innis-gloria rang for the Mass, four white birds rose from the loch and flew to church, where they occupied daily a bench, sitting side by side and exhibiting the utmost reverence and devotion. Charmed at the piety of the birds, S. Brandan prayed for them, when they were transformed into children, were baptized, and then died.

In a Sclavonian legend, a youth was reposing in a forest. The wind sighed through the trees, filling him with a tender melancholy which could find no expression in words. Presently there fluttered through the branches a snowy swan, which alighted on his breast. The youth clasped the beautiful bird to his heart, and resisted all its struggles to escape. Then the swan changed into a beautiful girl, who forthwith accompanied him to church, where they were united.

A weird Icelandic saga tells of a battle fought on the ice of Lake Vener, between two Swedish kings, assisted by the chief Helgi and King Olaf of Norway, supported by Hromund Greipsson, the betrothed of the king's sister Swan-white. Above the heads of the combatants flew a great swan; this was Kara, the mistress of Helgi, who had transformed herself into a bird. She, by her incantations, blunted the weapons of King Olaf's men, so that they began to give way before the Swedes. But accidentally Helgi, in raising his sword, smote off the leg of the swan which floated on expanded wings above his head. From that moment the tide of battle turned, and the Norwegians were victorious.

It is a fair subject for inquiry, whether the popular iconography of the angel-hosts is not indebted to the heathen myth for its most striking features. Our delineations of angels in flowing white robes, with large pinions, are derived from the later Greek and Roman representations of victory; but were not these figures – half bird, half woman – derived from the Apsaras of the Vedas, who were but the fleecy clouds, supposed in the ages of man's simplicity to be celestial swans?

CHAPTER 11

The Knight of the Swan

HE STORY under consideration here derives from two distinct sources. The first of these is the myth of the Swan-Children, of which we have already heard something in the preceding chapter. Versions of this story appear in Hebrew, Syriac, Greek, Persian, Arabic and Old Spanish, while the story of Helyas owes a good deal to the account of the ancient Irish tale of the Children of Lir. The second part of the story draws upon numerous versions of the mysterious boat pulled by a swan, some of which, once again, have been referred to in Chapter 10.

In places the story reads more like a faery-tale than an epic romance, with the theme of the children left in the wood and the replacement of babies with puppies; even the bad step-mother, Matabrunn, has her counterpart in numberless characters of this type found in faery- and folk-tales from many lands.

These factors suggest a more ancient point of origin for the tale, since most faery-tales circulated in aural tradition for many years before achieving a literary form.

Versions of the theme that involve a lady seeking a champion to defend her right in battle appear frequently throughout medieval romances. They include Lancelot defending the honour of Guinevere (and indeed Lancelot defending the rights of numerous ladies), Gawain defending the Lady of Lys in one of the Continuations of Chrétien de Troyes's *Perceval*, Gareth defeating all comers in defence of the rights of the Lady Lioness in Malory's *Morte D'Arthur*, Tristan defending Iseult in most versions of their story, and a vast number of less well-known knights following the oath of the Round Table to 'always to do ladies, damosels and gentlewomen succour . . . '

The prohibition which both Lohengrin and Helyas lay upon their respective wives is, of course, the same as that usually placed upon the partners of the faery women discussed in Chapters 8 and 10. Once their origin is known they are bound to return home, in most cases never to be seen again. One wonders at the reason for this. Perhaps it is simply that the Otherworldly beings fear retribution once their non-human origin is revealed; given the persecution meted out to anyone who showed any unusual abilities in the Middle Ages this would not be surprising. It seems as though there is an Otherworldly law operating here as well – those who are born in the Otherworld may only sojourn in this world as long as their secret is kept.

There is also an element of the initiation test: the human partner must resist the temptation to ask the fateful question. The latter is a curious reversal of the Grail story, where the asking of a ritual question brings healing to the Wounded King and the Waste Lands (see Chapter 12) while here, given Lohengrin's connection with the Family of the Grail, the question prompts him to depart and return whence he came. Richard Wagner must have asked this same question, because in his opera based on the legend he makes Lohengrin give a reason for his departure – this being that the Grail grants magical powers to its servants as long as they do not reveal the source of their power.

Another theme common to most of the Swan-Knight tales is, of course, the genealogy which accompanies them. It seems as though half the crowned heads of Europe could claim descent from an Otherworldly source, though as in the case of Melusine (Chapter 8) this could be seen to reflect badly upon the recipient of such 'tainted' blood. It should also be noted that in most instances the story itself is recorded retrospectively, as if to explain the nature of the family. Certainly in the case of the Lusignan line, this seems to have been so.

Another romance records that, after leaving Elsa, Lohengrin went on to marry Princess Belaye of Lizaborye but was murdered by soldiers sent by her parents, who believed that he had somehow enchanted their daughter. Belaye died of grief and the name of the country was changed to Lothringen (Lorraine). One of the major sources for the story of Helyas, not mentioned by Gould, is a thirteenth-century romance called *Dolopathus*, named after the king of Sicily who is here the father of the future Swan-Knight. The story told at the beginning of this work is almost exactly that of the Swan-Children except that no names are given to the seven children. The title of the section dealing with these events is 'Cygni Eques', 'The Knight of the Swan', and here, as in the versions discussed by Gould, one of the children cannot be changed back from his swan-shape because his collar has been lost. The collar bears the words: 'This is the swan whose name lasts forever, because with a golden chain it draws an armed soldier in a little boat.' Thus the legend of the Swan-Children, already current orally, is coupled with the legend of the Swan-Knight – the latter story being referred to in such a way as to suggest that it was already well known and so did not require extended reference.

An interesting example of the way that sources and stories can become confused is provided by the statue of the Swan-Knight to be found in the city of Cleve, the setting for the Helyas tale. The statue was erected in 1882 and depicts the knight holding a horn in his right hand while with his left he caresses the head of the swan. The statue is commonly known as 'the Lohengrin Monument' and is referred to by this title in guidebooks of the area, yet on the pedestal beneath the figure of the knight are four figures in bas-relief which bear the names Beatrix, Dietrich, Conrad and Gottfried – those of the protagonists in the Helyas story! Thus the two originally separate stories have become confused, and have acquired a common origin due to this lapse in the folk-memory of the site.

It has been suggested that one strand in the story may have derived from an actual historical figure: Roger de Toeni, whose granddaughter married into the family of Godfrey de Bouillon. This Roger, who died around 1040, was a man of prowess, and in the course of his knightly adventures went to Spain, freed the widowed Countess of Barcelona, married her daughter, and on his return to Normandy founded the Abbey of Châtillon near the town of Conches. It is said that Roger's emblem was the swan, and that he liked to be called the Swan-Knight. Whether this choice of name reflects a knowledge of the Lohengrin or Helyas story, or whether these were in turn influenced by the life and title of Roger we cannot say, but there may well be some borrowing in either direction.

*　　*　　*

'WE REDE in the auncient and autentike cronicles that sometime ther was a noble king in Lilefort, otherwise named the strong yle, a muche riche lande, the which kinge had to name Pieron. And he tooke to wife and spouse Matabrunne the doughter of an other king puissaunt and riche mervailously.' By his wife Matabrune, the king became father of Oriant, 'the which after the dyscease of his father abode with his mother as heir of the realme, whiche he succeded and governed peasiabli without to be maried.'

One day King Oriant chased a hart in the forest, and lost his way; exhausted with his ride, he drew rein near a fountain which bubbled out from under a mossy rock.

'And there he sat downe under a tree, to the which he reined his horse the better to solace and sporte him at his owne pleasure. And thus as he was in consolacion there came to him a yonge damoysel moche grevous and of noble maintene, named Beatrice, accompanied of a noble knight, and two squires, with iiii damoyselles, the which she held in her service and famyliarite.'

This Beatrice became the wife of Oriant, much to the chagrin of his mother, who had hitherto held rule in the palace, and who at once hated her daughter-in-law, and determined on her destruction.

The king had not been married many months before war broke out, and he was called from home to head his army. Before leaving, he consigned his wife to the care of his mother, who promised to guard her with the utmost fidelity. 'Whan the time limited and ordeined of almighti god approached that the noble and goodly quene Beatrice should be delivered after the cours of nature, the false matrone aforsaid went and delibered in herselfe to execute and put in effecte her malignus or moste wicked purpose. . . . But she comen made maners of great welth to the said noble quene Beatrice. And sodainly in great paine and traivable of bodye, she childed vi sonnes and a faire doughter, at whose birthe eche of them brought a chaine of silver about their neckes issuing out of their mothers wombe. And whan Matabrune saw the vii litle children borne having echone a chaine of silver at necke, she made them lightli and secretli to be borne a side by her chamberer of her teaching, and than toke vii litle dogges that she had prepared, and all bloudy laide them under the quene in manner as they had issued of her bodye.'

Then Matabrune ordered her squire Marks to take the seven children to the river and drown them; but the man, moved by compassion, left them in the forest on his cloak, where they were found by a hermit who 'toke and lapped them tenderly in his mantel and with al their chaines at their neckes he bare them into the litle hous of his hermitage, and there he warmed and sustened them of his poore goodnes as well as he coulde.' Of these children, one excelled the others in beauty. The pious old man baptized the little babes, and called the one who surpassed the others by the name Helias. 'And whan that they were in the age of theyr pleasaunt and fresshe grene yougth thei reane all about sporting and playinge in the said forest about the trees and floures.'

One day it fell out that a yeoman of Queen Matabrune, whilst chasing in the forest, saw the seven children sitting under a tree eating wild apples, each with a silver chain about his neck. Then he told Matabrune of the marvel he had seen, and she at once concluded that these were her grandchildren; wherefore she bade the yeoman take seven fellows with him and slay the children. But by the grace of God these men's hearts were softened, and, instead of murdering the little ones, they robbed them of their silver chains. But they only found six children, for the hermit had taken Helias with him on a begging excursion. Now, 'as soone as their chaines were of, they were al transmued in an instaunt in faire white swannes by the divine grace, and began to flee in the ayre through the forest, making a piteous and lamentable crye.'

Helias grew up with his godfather in the forest. The story goes on to relate how that the hermit was told by an angel in vision whose the children were; how a false charge was brought against Beatrice, and she was about to be executed, when Helias appeared in the lists, and by his valour proclaimed her innocence; and how Matabrune's treachery was discovered.

'But for to returne to the subject of the crony-kill of the noble Helias knight of the swanne. It is to be noted that the said Helias knight of the swanne demanded of Kyng Oriant his father that it wolde please him to give him the chaines of silver of his brethern and sister that the goldesmith had brought. The which he delivered him with good herte for to dispose them at his pleasure. Than he made an othe and sware that he wolde never rest tyll he had so longe sought by pondes and stagnes that he had founde his v brethren and his sister, which were transmued into swannes. But our Lorde that consoleth his freendes in exaltinge their good will shewed greatly his vertue. For in the river that ranne about the kinges palays appeared visibly the swannes before all the people. – And incontinent the kynge and the queene descended wyth many lordes, knightes, and gentilmen, and came with great diligence upon the water syde, for to see the above sayde swannes. The king and the queene behelde them piteousli in weeping for sorrow that they had to se theyr poore children so transmued into swannes. And whan they saw the good Helias come nere them they began to make a mervaylous feast and rejoyced them in the water. So he approched upon the brinke: and whan they sawe him nere them, they came lightli fawning and flickering about him making him chere, and he playned lovingly their fethers. After he shewed them the chaynes of silver, whereby they set them in good ordre before him. And to five of them he remised the chaynes about their neckes, and sodeynlye they began to retourne to theyr propre humayne forme as they were before.' But unfortunately the sixth chain had been melted to form a silver goblet, and therefore one of the brothers was unable to regain his human shape.

Helias spent some time with his father; but a voice within his breast called him to further adventures.

'After certayne tyme that the victoryous kynge Helyas had posseded the Realme of Lylefort in good peace and tranquilite of justice, it happened on a day as he was in his palais looking towarde the river that he apperceived the swanne, one of his brethren that was not yet tourned into his fourme humayne, for that his chaine was molten for to make Matabrune a cup. And the sayd swanne was in the water before a ship, the which he had led to the wharfe as abiding king Helias. And when Helias saw him, he saide in himselfe: Here is a signification that God sendeth to me for to shew to me that I ought to go by the guyding of this swanne into some countrey for to have honour and consolacion.

'And when Helyas had mekelye taken his leave of all his parentes and freendes, he made to bere his armures and armes of honoure into the shyppe, with hys target and his bright sheelde, of whiche as it is written the felde was of sylver, and thereon a double cross of golde. So descended anon the sayd Helyas with his parentes and freendes, the which came to convey him unto the brinke of the water.'

About this time, Otho, Emperor of Germany, held court at Neumagen, there to decide between Clarissa, Duchess of Bouillon, and the Count of Frankfort, who claimed her duchy. It was decided that their right should be established by single combat. The Count of Frankfort was to appear in person in the lists, whilst the duchess was to provide some doughty warrior who would do battle for her.

'Than the good lady as all abasshed loked aboute her if there were ony present that in her need wolde helpe her. But none wolde medle seynge the case to her imposed. Wherefore she committed her to God, praying Him humbly to succour her, and reprove the injury that wickedly to her was imposed by the sayd erle.'

The council broke up, and lords and ladies were scattered along the banks of the Meuse.

> So, as they stray'd, a swan they saw
>   Sail stately up and strong,
> And by a silver chain she drew
>   A little boat along,
> Whose streamer to the gentle breeze,
>   Long floating, flutter'd light,
> Beneath whose crimson canopy
>   There lay reclined a knight.
>
> With arching crest and swelling breast
>   On sail'd the stately swan,
> And lightly up the parting tide
>   The little boat came on.
> And onward to the shore they drew,
>   And leapt to land the knight,
> And down the stream the little boat
>   Fell soon beyond the sight.
>   SOUTHEY's *Rudiger*.

Of course this knight, who is Helias, fights the Count of Frankfort, overcomes him, and wins the heart of the daughter of the duchess. Thus Helias became Duke of Bouillon.

But before marrying the lady, he warned her that if she asked his name, he would have to leave her.

At the end of nine months, the wife of Helias gave birth to a daughter, who was named Ydain at the font, and who afterwards became the mother of Godfrey de Bouillon, King of Jerusalem, and of his brothers Baldwin and Eustace.

One night the wife forgot the injunction of her husband, and began to ask him his name and kindred. Then he rebuked her sorrowfully, and leaving his bed, bade her farewell. Instantly the swan reappeared on the river, drawing the little shallop after it, and uttering loud cries to call its brother. So Helias stepped into the boat, and the swan swam with it from the sight of the sorrowing lady.

The romance of Helias continues the story to the times of Godfrey de Bouillon, but I shall leave it at this point, as it ceases to deal with the myth which is the subject of this article. The story is very ancient and popular. It is told of Lohengrin, Loherangrin, Salvius, and Gerhard the Swan, whilst the lady is Beatrice of Cleves, or Else of Brabant. In the twelfth century it seems to have localized itself about the Lower Rhine.

Probably the most ancient mention of the fable is that of William of Tyre (1180), who says: 'We pass over, intentionally, the fable of the Swan, although many people regard it as a fact, that from it he (Godfrey de Bouillon) had his origin, because this story seems destitute of truth.' Next to him to speak of the story is Helinandus (circ. 1220), quoted by Vincent de Beauvais: 'In the diocese of Cologne, a famous and vast palace overhangs the Rhine, it is called Juvamen. Thither when once many princes were assembled, suddenly there came up a skiff, drawn by a swan attached to it by a silver chain. Then a strange and unknown knight leaped out before all, and the swan returned with the boat. The knight afterwards married, and had children. At length, when dwelling in this palace, he saw the swan return again with the boat and chain: he at once re-entered the vessel, and was never seen again; but his progeny remain to this day.'

A genealogy of the house of Flanders, in a MS of the thirteenth century, states: 'Eustachius venit ad Buillon ad domum ducissæ, quæ uxor erat militis, qui vocabatur miles Cigni.' Jacob van Maerlant (b. 1235), in his 'Spieghel Historiael', alludes to it –

> Logenaers niesdaet an doen,
> Dat si hem willen tien ane,
> Dat tie ridder metter swane
> Siere moeder vader was.
> No wijt no man, als ict vernam
> Ne was noint swane, daer hi af quam
> Als ist dat hem Brabanters beroemen
> Dat si van der Swane siin coemen.

And Nicolaes de Klerc, who wrote in 1318, thus refers to it in his 'Brabantine Gests': 'Formerly the Dukes of Brabant have been much belied in that it is said of them that they came with a swan.' And Jan Veldenar (1480) says: 'Now, once upon a time, this

noble Jungfrau of Cleves was on the banks by Nymwegen, and it was clear weather, and she gazed up the Rhine, and saw a strange sight: for there came sailing down a white swan with a gold chain about its neck, and by this it drew a little skiff . . . ' – and so on.

There is an Icelandic saga of Helis, the Knight of the Swan, translated from the French by the Monk Robert, in 1226. In the Paris royal library is a romance upon this subject, consisting of about 30,000 lines, begun by a Renax or Renant, and finished by a Gandor de Douay. In the British Museum is a volume of French romances, containing, among others, 'L'Ystoire du Chevalier au Signe', told in not less than 3000 lines.

The 'Chevelere Assigne', a shorter poem on the same subject, was reprinted by M. Utterson for the Roxburghe Club, from a MS in the Cottonian library, which has been quoted by Percy and Warton as an early specimen of alliterative versification. It is certainly not later than the reign of Henry VI.

The next prose romance of Helias is that of Pierre Desrey, entitled 'Les faictz et gestes du preux Godsffroy de Boulion, aussi plusieurs croniques et histoires'; Paris, without date. 'La Genealogie avecques les gestes et nobles faitz darmes du tres preux et renomme prince Godeffroy de Boulion: et de ses chevalereux freres Baudo et Eustace: yssus et descendus de la tres noble et illustre lignee du vertueux Chevalier au Cyne'; Paris, Jean Petit, 1504; also Lyons, 1580. This book was partly translated into English, and printed by Wynkyn de Worde, 'The hystory of Hilyas Knight of the Swann, imprynted by Wynkyn de Worde', &c., 1512; and in full by Caxton, under the title, 'The last Siege and Conqueste of Jherusalem, with many histories therein comprised'; Westmester, fol. 1480.

It is from the first thirty-eight chapters of the French 'Faits et Gestes', that Robert Copland translated his Helias, which he dedicated 'to the puyssant and illustrious prynce, lorde Edwarde, duke of Buckynghame', because he was lineally descended from the Knight of the Swan. This duke was beheaded, May 17th, 1521.

We need hardly follow the story in other translations.

The romance, as we have it, is a compilation of at least two distinct myths. The one is that of the Swan-children, the other of the Swan-knight. The compiler of the romance has pieced the first legend to the second, in order to explain it. In its original form, the knight who came to Neumagen, or Cleves, in the swan-led boat, and went away again, was unaccounted for: who he was, no man knew; and Heywood, in his 'Hierarchies of the blessed Angels', 1635, suggests that he was one of the evil spirits called *incubi*; but the romancer solved the mystery by prefixing to the story of his marriage with the duchess a story of transformation, similar to that of Fionmala, referred to in the previous article.

We shall put aside the story of the swan-children and confine our attention to the genuine myth.

The home of the fable was that border-land where Germans and Kelts met, where the Nibelungen legends were brought in contact with the romances of Arthur and the Sangreal.

Lohengrin belongs to the round table; the hero who releases Beatrice of Cleves is called Elias Grail. Pighius relates that in ancient annals it is recorded that Elias came from the blessed land of the earthly paradise, which is called Graele. And the name Helias, Helius, Elis, or Salvius, is but a corruption of the Keltic ala, eala, ealadh, a swan. I believe the story of the Knight of the Swan to be a myth of local Brabantine

129

origin. That it is not the invention of the romancer is evident from the variations in the tale, some of which we must now consider.

1. Lohengrin.

The Duke of Limburg and Brabant died leaving an only daughter, Else or Elsam. On his death-bed he committed her to the care of Frederick von Telramund, a brave knight, who had overcome a dragon in Sweden. After the duke's death, Frederick claimed the hand of Else, on the plea that it had been promised him; but when she refused it, he appealed to the emperor, Henry the Fowler, asking permission to assert his right in the lists against any champion Else might select.

Permission was granted, and the duchess looked in vain for a knight who would fight in her cause against the redoubted Frederick of Telramund.

Then, far away, in the sacred temple of the Grail, at Montsalvatsch, tolled the bell, untouched by human hands, a signal that help was needed. At once Lohengrin, son of Percival, was sent to the rescue, but whither to go he knew not. He stood foot in stirrup, ready to mount, when a swan appeared on the river drawing a ship along. No sooner did Lohengrin behold this, than he exclaimed: 'Take back the horse to its stable; I will go with the bird whither it shall lead!'

Trusting in God, he took no provision on board. After he had been five days on the water, the swan caught a fish, ate half, and gave the other half to the knight.

In the mean while the day of ordeal approached, and Else fell into despair. But at the hour when the lists were opened, there appeared the boat drawn by the silver swan; and in the little vessel lay Lohengrin asleep upon his shield. The swan drew the boat to the landing, the knight awoke, sprang ashore, and then the bird swam away with the vessel.

Lohengrin, as soon as he heard the story of the misfortunes of the Duchess Else, undertook to fight for her. The knight of the Grail prevailed, and slew Frederick. Then Else surrendered herself and her duchy to him; but he would only accept her hand on condition that she should not ask his race. For some time they lived together happily. One day, in a tournament, he overthrew the Duke of Cleves and broke his arm, whereat the Duchess of Cleves exclaimed: 'This Lohengrin may be a strong man and a Christian, but who knows whence he has sprung!' These words reached the ears of the Duchess of Brabant; she coloured and hung her head.

At night, Lohengrin heard her sobbing. He asked: 'My love, what ails thee?'

She replied: 'The Duchess of Cleves has wounded me.'

Lohengrin asked no more.

Next night she wept again; her husband again asked the reason, and received the same answer.

On the third night she burst forth with: 'Husband, be not angry, but I must know whence you have sprung.'

Then Lohengrin told her that his father was Percival, and that God had sent him from the custody of the Grail. And he called his children to him, and said, kissing them: 'Here are my horn and my sword, keep them carefully; and here, my wife, is the ring my mother gave me – never part with it.'

Now, at break of day, the swan reappeared on the river, drawing the little shallop. Lohengrin re-entered the boat, and departed never to return.

Such is the story in the ancient German poem of Lohengrin, published by Görres from a MS in the Vatican; and in the great Percival of Wolfram von Eschenbach, verses 24,614–24,715.

2. The swan-knight of Conrad von Würzburg resembles Lohengrin and Helias in the outline of the story, but no name is given to the hero. He marries the daughter of the deceased Duke Gottfried of Brabant, and fights against the Duke of Saxony. His children are the ancestors of the great houses of Gelders and Cleves, which bear a swan as their arms.

3. Gerard Swan

One day Charlemagne stood at his window over-looking the Rhine. Then he was ware of a swan floating on the water, drawing a boat by a silken band fastened round its neck. When the boat came alongside of the quay, the swan ceased to row, and the emperor saw that a knight armed cap-a-pie sat in the skiff, and round his neck hung a ribbon to which was attached a note. Navilon (Nibelung), one of the emperor's men, gave the stranger his hand to help him out of the bark, and conducted him to Charlemagne. The monarch inquired of the stranger his name; for answer he pointed to the letter on his breast. This the king read. It stated that Gerard Swan sought a wife and lands.

Navilon then unarmed the strange knight, and the king gave him a costly mantle. So they went to table. But when Roland observed the man, he asked who he was. Charlemagne replied, 'He is a godsend'; and Roland observed, 'He seems to be a man of courage.'

Gerard proved to be a worthy knight; he served the monarch well. He soon learned to talk. The king was very fond of him, and gave him his sister Adalis in marriage, and made him Duke of Ardennes.

4. Helias.

In the year 711 lived Beatrice only daughter of Dietrich, Duke of Cleves, at her castle of Nymwegen. One bright day she sat at her window looking down the Rhine, when she saw a swan drawing a boat by a gold chain. In this vessel was Helias. He came ashore, won her heart, became Duke of Cleves, and lived happily with her for many years. One thing alone interfered with her happiness: she knew not whence her husband came, and he had strictly forbidden her to ask. But once she broke his command, and asked him whence he had come to her. Then he gave his children his sword, his horn, and his ring, bidding them never separate or lose these legacies, and entering the boat which returned for him, he vanished for ever. One of the towers of Cleves is called, after this event, the Swan-tower, and is surmounted by a swan.

5. Salvius Brabo.

Gottfried-Carl was King of Tongres, and lived at Megen on the Maas. He had a son named Carl-Ynach, whom he banished for some misdemeanour. Carl-Ynach fled to Rome, where he fell in love with Germana, daughter of the Proconsul Lucius Julius, and fled with her from the eternal city. They took ship to Venice, whence they travelled on horseback to Burgundy, and reached Cambray. Thence they proceeded to a place called Senes, and finding a beautiful valley, they dismounted to repose. Here a swan, at which one of the servants aimed an arrow, took refuge in the arms of Germana, who, delighted at the incident, asked Carl-Ynach the name of the bird in his native tongue. He replied 'Swana.' 'Then,' said she, 'let me be henceforth called by that name, lest, if I keep my former name, I be recognized and parted from thee.'

The lady took the swan with her as they proceeded on their journey, and fed it from her hand.

They now reached Florimont, near Brussels, and there Carl-Ynach heard that his father was dead. He was therefore King of Tongres. Shortly after his arrival at

Megen, his wife gave birth to a son, whom he named Octavian, and next year to a daughter, whom they called Swan. Shortly after, Ariovistus, King of the Saxones, waged war against Julius Cæsar. Carl Ynach united his forces with those of Ariovistus, and fell in the battle of Besançon. Swan, his widow, then fled with his children and her husband's body to Megen, fearing her brother Julius Cæsar. There she buried Carl-Ynach, and daily fed her swan upon his grave.

In the Roman army was a hero, Salvius Brabon by name, descended from Frankus, son of Hector of Troy. Cæsar rested at Cleves, and Salvius Brabon amused himself with shooting birds in the neighbourhood. One day he wandered to the banks of the Rhine. On its discoloured waters swam a snow-white swan, playfully pulling at the rope which bound a small skiff to the shore. Salvius leaped into the boat, and cast it loose from its mooring. Then the bird swam before him as a guide, and he rowed after it. On reaching the castle of Megen, the swan rose from the water, and flew to the grave of Carl-Ynach, where its mistress was wont to feed it. Salvius pursued it, bow in hand, and was about to discharge an arrow, when a window of the castle opened, and a lady cried to him in Latin to spare the bird. Salvius consented; and casting aside his bow and arrow, entered the castle. There he learned the story of the lady. He hastened to Julius Cæsar, and told him that his sister was in the neighbourhood. The conqueror accompanied Salvius to the castle, and embraced Germana with joy. Salvius Brabon then asked the emperor to give him the young damsel Swan in marriage, and he readily complied with the request, creating him at the same time Duke of Brabant; Octavian took the name of Germanicus, and became King of Cologne, and Tongres exchanged its name for Germania, after the sister of the emperor, its queen.

It was in commemoration of the beautiful myth of the Swan-knight, that Frederick II of Brandenburg instituted the Order of the Swan, in 1440. The badge was a chain from which was suspended an image of the Virgin, and underneath that a swan. The badge of the Cleves order of knighthood was also a silver swan suspended from a gold chain. In 1453, Duke Adolph of Cleves held a tournament at Lille, 'au nom du Chevalier au Cygne, serviteur des dames'.

On the 13th May, 1548, the Count of Cleves presented the players with a silver swan of considerable value. Charles, Duke of Cleves, attempted, in 1615, to revive the order of the swan. When Cleves fell to Prussia, the Court de Bar endeavoured to persuade Frederick the Great to resuscitate the order, but in vain. With Anne of Cleves, the white swan passed to our tavern signboards.

The myth is a Belgic religious myth. Just as in the Keltic legends of the Fortunate Isles, we hear of mortals who went by ship to the Avalon of Spirits, and then returned to their fellow-mortals; so in this Belgic fable we have a denizen of the distant paradise coming by boat to this inhabited land, and leaving it again.

In the former legends the happy mortal lives in the embraces of a divine being in perpetual youth; in the latter, a heavenly being unites himself, for a while, to a woman of earth, and becomes the ancestor of an aristocracy.

An Anglo-Saxon story bears some traces of the same legend. A ship once arrived on the coast of Scandia, without rudder or sail; in it lay a boy asleep upon his arms. The natives took and educated him, calling him Scild, the son of Sceaf (the skiff). In course of time he became their king. In Beowulf, it is added that Scild reigned long; and when he saw that he was about to die, he bade his men lay him fully armed in a boat, and thrust him out to sea. Among the Norse such a practice was not unknown. King Haki, when he died, was laid in a ship, the vessel fired, and sent out upon the waves. And the same is told of Baldur. But the shipping of the dead had no significance in Scandinavian mythology, whilst it was full of meaning in that of the Kelts. The Scandinavian Valhalla was not situated beyond the Western Sea, but on the summit of a great mountain; whereas the Keltic Avalon lay over the blue waters, beneath the setting sun. Consequently, I believe the placing of the dead in ships to have been a practice imported among the Northern and Germanic nations, and not indigenous.

The classic fable of Helios sailing in his golden vessel deserves notice in connexion with the myth of Helias. That the sun and moon travel in boats of silver or gold is an idea common to many mythologies. At first sight it seems probable that Helias is identical with Helios; but the difficulty of explaining how this classic deity should have become localized in Brabant is insurmountable, and I prefer the derivation of the name Helias from the Keltic appellation of the swan.

The necessity of the knight leaving his bride the moment she inquired his race connects this story with the Grail myth. According to the rules of the order of the Sangreal, every knight was bound to return to the temple of the order, immediately that any one asked his lineage and office. In the popular legend this reason does not appear, because the Grail was a genuine Keltic myth, with its roots in the mysteries of Druidism.

CHAPTER 12

The Sangreal

T HE MYTHS of the Grail form the centrepiece of the Arthurian tradition from the twelfth century onwards. Chrétien de Troyes, a poet attached to the court of Count Philip of Flanders, began his last work around 1180. Entitled *The Story of the Graal*, it told of an innocent youth named Perceval brought up in ignorance of the ways of men, who found his way to Arthur's court and from there embarked upon an extraordinary adventure in search of the Grail. Chrétien died before he could complete the story and the way was left open to others to finish it for him. Three other writers took up the tale, adding new characters and adventures and fresh clues as to the origin and meaning of the mysterious Grail. From here onward the story developed at an astonishing rate, with fresh versions appearing every year throughout the twelfth and thirteenth centuries. The original hero, Perceval, was joined by two companions, one of whom, Galahad, soon ousted him to become the first of the Quest knights to achieve the mystery of the Grail. Dindrane, Perceval's sister, had a vision of the Grail before any of her masculine counterparts and joined them in the search.

New works appeared which began to trace the earlier history of this most sacred of relics. A scribal error which misread San Greal (Holy Grail) as Sang Real (Holy Blood) caused it to be identified with the cup used by Jesus to celebrate the Last Supper and subsequently with the vessel in which Joseph of Arimathea (Christ's 'uncle' according to apocryphal tradition) collected some of Jesus's blood as the body was prepared for burial. Once caught up in the machinery of Christian relic-hunting, the fame of the Grail was assured.

A vast set of romances preserved under the title of *The Vulgate Cycle* (or more recently *The Lancelot-Grail*) interpreted the whole story in theological terms, adding the tale of the Dolorous Blow, in which the Grail King receives a terrible wound that will not heal, which also causes the Waste Land – a tract of barren country where nothing will grow. This theme drew upon a very ancient Celtic belief in the sacredness of the land and the intimate bond forged between the ruler and the country over which he ruled. Only the successful Grail-winner could bring about the healing of both king and land.

The origins of these mysterious stories have been the subject of literally hundreds of books and studies, as well as of countless poems, plays and novels (and, more recently, films), each with its own interpretation, its own thesis and, depending on its author, its own belief system. The Grail has been described as a cup, a dish, a stone, a floating altar, a bloodline and an idea. It has been sought after, discovered, lost again, recovered again, but has refused to be codified or placed within a framework which could successfully contain it.

In essence it seems to have been a body of teaching, deriving ultimately from pre-Christian sources but subsequently Christianized and carried by word of mouth down the centuries by such bodies as the Order of the Knights Templar, the heretical sect of the Cathars, whose sober lifestyle certainly reflects that of the Grail knights. From there onward it passed into the keeping of various esoteric groups, who from time to time have claimed its physical presence, and who have enabled its mystery to flourish into our own time.

The origin of the Templar 'head' which Gould mentions may well have a basis in historical fact. A recent book suggested that the object in question may have been the Mandylion, a gilded reliquary containing the original shroud of Christ, folded so that only the face showed. This sacred relic seems to have been for a time in the possession of the Templars and could certainly account not only for the story of the worship of the head, but also for its connection with the Grail. Wolfram von Eschenbach, the twelfth-century German poet who embroidered considerably on the tale told by Chrétien, called the guardians of the Grail 'Templiessen', which has been seen as the origin of its association with the august body of Soldier-Monks.

Gould's remarks concerning the Welsh romance of *Bran* are curiously inaccurate for such a generally careful scholar. The Cauldron described in the romance was not destroyed by Bran flinging a severed head into it, but by his brother Evnissien hiding among the dead followers of their enemies on the field of battle. When the dead warriors were put into the Cauldron they came out alive again; when a living man was placed therein the Cauldron burst. Thus Gould's interesting theory regarding the origin of the Grail as a pagan receptacle intended for use in a religious ceremony does not entirely stand up – though in fact he came near to the truth in his recognition of the Grail's origin as a Celtic vessel. A poem written down in the ninth century, but originating several hundred years earlier, describes the voyage undertaken by Arthur and his warriors in search of the Cauldron of Annwn. It is this poem which represents a more ancient story which must have been circulating among the tales of Arthur for a long time before Chrétien de Troyes (or some other writer whose work no longer survives)

first wrote it down – and thus began a quest which still continues several centuries later and which shows no sign of coming to an end.

* * *

WHEN Sir Lancelot came to the palace of King Pelles, in the words of Sir Thomas Malory, 'either of them made much of other, and so they went into the castle for to take their repast. And anon there came in a dove at the window, and in her bill there seemed a little sencer of gold, and therewith there was such a savour as though all the spicery of the world had been there; and forthwith all there was upon the table all manner of meates and drinkes that they could thinke upon. So there came a damosell, passing faire and young, and she beare a vessell of gold betweene her hands, and thereto the king kneeled devoutly and said his prayers, and so did all that were there: "Oh, Jesu!" said Sir Lancelot, "what may this meane?"

'"This is," said King Pelles, "the richest thing that any man hath living; and when this thing goeth about, the round-table shall bee broken. And wit yee well," said King Pelles, "that this is the holy Sancgreall which yee have heere seene."'

The next to see the sacred vessel was the pious Sir Bors. And after that he had seen it, 'he was led to bed into a faire large chamber, and many doores were shut about that chamber. And when Sir Bors espied all those doores, he made all the people to avoide, for he might have no body with him; but in no wise Sir Bors would unarme him, but so laid him upon the bed. And right so he saw come in a light that he might wel see a speare great and long which come straight upon him pointlong. And so Sir Bors seemed that the head of the speare brent like a taper; and anon, or Sir Bors wist, the speare head smote him into the shoulder an hand breadth in deepness, and that wound grieved Sir Bors passing sore.'

One day, when King Arthur and his court were at Camelot, sitting at supper, 'anon they heard cracking and crying of thunder, that hem thought the place should all to-rive; in the midst of the blast entred a sunne-beame more clear by seaven times than ever they saw day, and all they were alighted by the grace of the Holy Ghost. Then began every knight to behold other, and either saw other by their seeming fairer than ever they saw afore, nor for then there was no knight that might speake any word a great while; and so they looked every man on other as they had been dombe. Then there entred into the hall the holy grale covered with white samite, but there was none that might see it, nor who beare it, and there was all the hall fulfilled with good odours, and every knight had such meate and drinke as he best loved in this world; and when the holy grale had beene borne through the hall, then the holy vessel departed suddenly, and they wist not where it became.'

Then the knights stood up in their places one after another, and vowed to go in quest of the Sangreal, and not to return to the round-table till they had obtained a full view of it.

We must leave the knights to start upon their quest, and turn, for the history of the Grail, to the romance of the San Greal, the Perceval of Chrétien de Troyes, written at the close of the twelfth century, and the Titurel and Parcival of Wolfram von Eschenbach, translated into German from romances older than that of Chrétien de Troyes.

When Christ was transfixed by the spear, there flowed from His side blood and water. Joseph of Arimathæa collected the blood in the vessel from which the Saviour had eaten the last supper. The enraged Jews cast Joseph into prison, and left him to die of hunger. But for forty-two years he lay in the dungeon nourished and invigorated by the sacred vessel which was in his possession. Titus released Joseph from prison, and received baptism at his hands. Then Joseph started with the vessel and the blood, or the Sangreal, for Britain. Before he died, he confided the sacred treasure to his nephew. But according to another version of the legend, the Grail was preserved in heaven, till there should appear on earth a race of heroes, worthy to become its guardians. The chief of this line was an Asiatic prince, named Perillus, who came to Gaul, where his descendants allied themselves with the family of a Breton prince. Titurel, who sprang from this heroic lineage, was the one chosen of God to found the worship of the Sangreal among the Gauls. Angels brought the vessel to him, and instructed him in its mysteries. He erected, on the model of the temple at Jerusalem, a magnificent temple to the Grail. He organized a band of guardians of the vessel, and elaborated the ceremonial of its worship. The Grail, we are told, was only visible to the baptized, and only partially if they were tainted by sin. To the pure in heart alone was it perfectly visible.

Every Good Friday a white dove descended from heaven, bearing a white oblation which it laid before the Grail. The holy vessel gave oracles, expressed miraculously in characters which appeared on the surface of the bowl, and then vanished. Spiritual blessings attended on the vision and custody of the sacred vessel; the guardians, and those who were privileged to behold it, were conscious of a mysterious internal joy, a foretaste of that of heaven. The material blessings are easier to be described. The Grail stood in the place of all food, it supplied its worshippers with the meats they most desired and the drinks most to their taste; it maintained them in perpetual youth. The day on which the Grail had been seen, its guardians were incapable of being wounded or suffering any hurt. If they fought for eight days after the vision, they were susceptible of wounds but not of death.

Every thing in the construction of the temple was full of mystery. It was erected on Montsalvatsch, of precious stones, gold, and aloe-wood. In form it was circular; there were three principal entrances. The knights who watched the Grail were patterns of virtue. All sensual love, even within the limits of marriage, was strictly forbidden. A single thought of passion would obscure the eye and conceal the mystic vessel. The chief of this order of knights was entitled King. As his office was hereditary, he was permitted to marry.

When the faith or the right was in jeopardy, a bell rang in the chapel of the Grail, and a knight was bound to go forth sword in hand to the defence. Wherever he was, should a question be asked him of his condition or office in the temple, he was to refuse to answer, and at once to return to Montsalvatsch.

Titurel reigned four hundred years, and he, to all appearances, seemed of the age of forty. He was succeeded in his office by his son Frimutelle, who transgressed, by loving a damsel, Floramie by name. Consequently he lost the grace of the holy Grail, and fell in a joust, engaged in to give pleasure and do honour to his mistress.

He was succeeded by his son Amfortas, who fell into grievous sin, and was given over by the Grail to be wounded by a lance. Then it was announced that he should not be healed of his wound till one came, pure and young, to Montsalvatsch who would see the mysteries of the sacred vessel, and ask their signification.

This Amfortas is the Pelles or Pellam of the 'Mort d'Arthure'.

138

Years passed, and the king lay wounded in his palace. The brotherhood of the Grail was dissolved, and the existence of the temple and its mystic rites was almost forgotten. Sir Thomas Malory gives a different account of the wounding of the king from that in the Romans du San Greal, and makes his healing depend on the arrival of a knight who is a 'clean maid', who shall apply to him the sacred blood.

In the fulness of time, Galahad, the Good Knight, came to king Arthur's court, and went forth, with the other knights, to the quest of the holy Grail.

Let us follow Launcelot who was on a ship.

'The winde arose and drove Sir Launcelot more than a moneth throughout the sea, where he slept but little and prayed unto God that he might have a sight of the Sancgreall. So it befell upon a night at midnight hee arived afore a castle on the backe side, which was rich and faire, and there was a posterne that opened toward the sea, and was open without any keeping, save two lions kept the entrie, and the moone shined cleare.

'Anon Sir Launcelot heard a voice that said, "Launcelot, goe out of this ship, and enter into the castle where thou shalt see a great part of thy desire." Then he ranne to his armes, and armed him, and so hee went unto the gate, and saw the two lions; then hee set hands to his sword and drew it; then came there sudainly a dwarfe, that smote him upon the arme so sone that the sword fell out of his hand. Then he heard a voice that said, "Oh man of evill faith and poore beliefe, wherefore believest thou more in thy harneis than in thy Maker? for Hee might more availe thee than thine armour, in whose service thou art set." – Then Sir Launcelot entered in so armed, and hee found no gate nor doore but it was opened. And so at the last he found a chamber whereof the doore was shut, and hee set his hands thereto for to have opened it, but hee might not. Then he enforced him much for to undoe the doore. Then he listened; and heard a voice which sung so sweetly, that it seemed none earthly thing, and him thought that the voice said, "Joy and honour be to the Father of heaven." Then Sir Launcelot kneeled downe before the chamber, for well he wist that there was the Sancgreall in that chamber. Then said he, "Faire sweete Father, Jesu Christ, if ever I did thing that pleased the Lord, for thy pittie ne have me not in despite for my foull sins done here before time, and that thou shew me some thing of that which I seek."

'And with that he saw the chamber door open, and there came out a great clearenesse, that the house was as bright as though all the torches of the world had beene there. So came hee to the chamber doore, and would have entered, and anon a voice said unto him, "Flee, Sir Launcelot, and enter not, for thou oughtest not to doe it, and if thou enter thou shalt forethinke it." And hee withdrew him back, and was right heavie in his mind.

'Then looked hee up in the midst of the chamber, and saw a table of silver, and the holy vessel covered with red samite, and many angels about it, whereof one of them held a candell of waxe burning, and the other held a crosse, and the ornaments of the altar. And before the holy vessell he saw a good man clothed like a priest, and it seemed that hee was at the sakering of the masse; and it seemed unto Sir Launcelot that above the priest's hands there were three men, whereof the two put the youngest by likeness betweene the priest's hands, and so hee lift it up on high, and it seemed to shew so to the people. And then Sir Launcelot mervailed not a little, for him thought that the priest was so greatly charged of the figure, that him seemed that heem should have fallen to the ground; and when hee saw none about him that

139

would helpe him, then hee came to the doore a great pace – and entred into the chamber, and came toward the table of silver; and when he came nigh he felt a breath, that him thought was intermedled with fire, which smote him so sore in the visage that him thought it all to-brent his visage, and therewith hee fell to the ground, and had no power to arise.'

Sir Galahad, Sir Percival, and Sir Bors met in the forest, and rode together to the castle of King Pelles. There they supped, and after supper they beheld a great light, and in the light were four angels bearing up an ancient man in bishop's vestments, and they set him down before a table of silver, on which appeared the Sangreal. And this aged prelate was Joseph of Arimathæa, 'the first bishop of Christendom'. Then other angels appeared bearing candles, and a spear from which fell drops of blood, and these drops were collected by an angel in a box. Then the angels set the candles upon the table, and 'the fourth set the holy sphere even upright upon the vessel,' as represented on an ancient churchyard crucifix, in rude sculpture, at Sancreed, in Cornwall.

Joseph next celebrated the sacred mysteries, and, at the consecration, our Blessed Lord appeared and said, 'Galahad, sonne, wotest thou what I hold between My hands?' 'Nay,' replied the maiden knight, 'but if yee tell mee.' 'This is,' He said, 'the holy dish wherein I eate the lambe on Sher-Thursday, and now hast thou seene that thou desirest most to see, but yet hast thou not seene it so openly as thou shalt see it in the citie of Sarras, in the spirituall place. Therefore thou must goe hence, and beare with thee this holy vessell, for this night it shall depart from the realme of Logris, that it shall never be seen more heere.'

So Galahad, after having anointed the wounded king with the blood which dropped from the spear, and made him whole, departed with his friends Bors and Perceval to the mystic city of Sarras, where he was made king.

The story is somewhat different in the Perceval of Chrétien de Troyes. This romance was commenced by Chrétien at the request of Phillip of Alsace, Count of Flanders; it was continued by Gauthier de Denet, and finished by Manessier, towards the close of the twelfth century. It is the history of the quest of the San Greal.

Perceval was the son of a poor widow in Wales, brought up by her in a forest, far removed from all warlike images. One day he saw a knight ride past, and from that moment he had no rest, till his mother gave him arms and let him ride to the court of King Arthur. On his way he saw a tent in which lay a beautiful damsel asleep. Perceval took the ring from her finger, ate and drank at the table which was spread in the tent, and then pursued his course. As he entered the court at Cardueil, a felon knight stole the goblet from the king's table. Perceval went in pursuit. One evening he entered a castle where lay a sick king on a couch. The door of the hall opened, and there came in a servant bearing a bleeding lance, others with golden candlesticks, and finally the holy Grail. Perceval asked no questions, and was reproached on his leaving the castle for not making inquiries into the mystery of the Grail. Afterwards he undertook the quest of this marvellous vessel, but had great difficulty in finding again the castle of the wounded king. When his search was crowned with success, he asked the signification of the mystic rite which took place before his eyes, and was told that the king was a Fisher, descended from Joseph of Arimathæa, and uncle of Perceval; that the spear was that which had pierced the Saviour's side, and that the Grail was the vessel in which the sacred blood of Christ had been collected. The king had been wounded in trying to mend a sword which had been broken by a knight named Pertinax, and which could only be welded together by a knight without fear and reproach. The Fisher-king would recover health only when Pertinax died. On hearing this, Perceval sought out and slew Pertinax, healed his uncle, obtained in return the sacred vessel and the bleeding lance, and retired to a hermitage. On his death –

> Fut au ciel remis sans doutance
> Et le Saint-Graal et la Lance.

It is very certain that Chrétien de Troyes was not the inventor of this mystic tale, for there exists in the 'Red Book' a Welsh tale entitled Pheredur, which is indisputably the original of Perceval.

The 'Red Book' is a volume of Welsh prose and verse romances and tales, begun in the year 1318, and finished in 1454. It is preserved in the library of Jesus College, Oxford. Although Pheredur was transcribed after Perceval was composed, it bears evidence of a higher antiquity.

Pheredur is not a Christian. His habits are barbarous. The Grail is not a sacred Christian vessel, but a mysterious relic of a past heathen rite. The same incidents occur in Perceval as in Pheredur, but in the former they are modified and softened, and various points indicative of barbarism and paganism are omitted.

Pheredur enters a castle, and 'Whilst he and his uncle were discoursing together, they beheld two young men entering the hall, bearing a lance of unusual length, from the point of which distilled three gouts of gore; and when the company beheld this, they began to wail and lament. But the old man continued to talk with Pheredur; and as he did not tell Pheredur the reason of what took place, Pheredur did not venture to ask him. And when the cries ceased, there entered two damsels with a basin in which was the head of a man swimming in blood. Then the company uttered a piercing wail.'

In the Perceval, and in the Mort d'Arthure, the head is omitted, and to the lance and grail are attributed a Christian value; but in the Pheredur there is no trace whatever of these symbols having any Christian signification.

Pheredur signifies, according to M. de la Villemarqué, 'The Companion of the Basin', and is a synonym of Perceval; Per being a basin, and Këval and Këdur having alike the meaning of companion.

Pheredur is mentioned as well in the Annales Cambriæ, which extend from the year 444 to 1066. Geoffrey of Monmouth also speaks of the reign of Peredure, 'who governed the people with generosity and mildness, so that he even excelled his other brothers who had preceded him'; and the anonymous author of the 'Life of Merlin' speaks of him as the companion and consoler of the bard. Aneurin, the contemporary of Hengst and Horsa, the author of the Gododin, terms him one of the most illustrious princes of the Isle of Britain.

Taliesin ben Beirdd, the famous poet of the same age, speaks of the sacred vessel in a manner which connects it with bardic mythology. 'This vessel,' he says, 'inspires poetic genius, gives wisdom, discovers the knowledge of futurity, the mysteries of the world, the whole treasure of human sciences.' And he describes it as adorned like the Grail, with a beading of pearls and diamonds. One of his poems contains the history of Bran the Blessed, in which the mystic vessel occupies a prominent position.

One day, whilst hunting in Ireland, Bran arrived on the banks of a lake, called the Lake of the Basin. He saw there a black and hideous giant, a witch, and a dwarf, rise from the water holding a vessel in their hands. He persuaded them to accompany him to Wales, where he lodged them in his palace, and in return for his hospitality, received the basin. This vase had the property of healing all mortal ills, of staunching blood, of resuscitating the dead. But those who were restored to life by it were not enabled to speak, lest they should divulge the mysteries of the vessel. At a banquet given by Bran to Martholone, King of Ireland, the Welsh prince presented the bowl to his guest. He regretted that he had made this present, when some years later war broke out between the King of Ireland and himself. Then he found himself unable to cope with his adversary, whose every slain soldier recovered life by means of the sacred vessel. But Bran smote off the head of a hostile chief, and cast the bloody head into the bowl, when it burst, and its virtues ceased.

This basin was reckoned as one of the thirteen wonders of the Isle of Britain, brought by Merdhyn, or Merlin, in his crystal ark. That it is the same as Ceridwen's cauldron is not improbable. Ceridwen was the Keltic Great Mother, the Demeter, the source of life, and the receptacle of the dead. The story of her cauldron is told in the Pair Ceridwen (vessel of Ceridwen), or Hanes Taliesin (History of Taliesin).

In ancient times there was a man, Tegid Voel by name, who had a wife called Ceridwen by whom he had a son Morvran ap Tegid, and a daughter Creirwy, both very beautiful; also Aragddu, the most hideous of beings. Ceridwen, knowing that the poor deformed child would have little joy of life, determined to prepare for him the Water of Inspiration. She placed a cauldron on a fire, filled it with the requisite ingredients, and left little Gwion to attend to its seething, and blind Morda to keep up the fire for a year and a day, without suffering the operation to cease for a moment. One day, near the end of the twelve-month, three drops spirted out of the bubbling liquid, and Gwion caught them on his finger. As they scalded him, he put his finger into his mouth, and at once obtained the knowledge of futurity. He saw that Ceridwen would attempt his death, in consequence of his having tasted the precious drops; so he prudently took to flight. Then the cauldron burst and extinguished the fire.

Ceridwen, in her rage, struck Morda on the head, and rushed in pursuit of Gwion the Little. He transformed himself into a hare; then she took the form of a hound. He sprang into a river and took that of a fish; instantly she became an otter. Then he rose from the water as a little bird; but she soared after him as a hawk. Then he dropped as a grain of wheat on a corn-heap; but Ceridwen, instantly taking the shape of a hen, swallowed him. She became pregnant thereby, and in nine months gave birth to a lovely child which she hid in a leather coracle and committed to the waves, on the 29th of April.

In this bardic tale we have certainly a very ancient Keltic myth. What the cauldron signifies it is difficult to ascertain. Some suppose it to represent the ocean, others the working of the vital force of earth, which produces the three seasons which are good, symbolized by the drops. But we know too little of druidic mythology, and those legends which have come to us have descended in a too altered form, for us to place much confidence in such conjectures.

But that this vessel of the liquor of Wisdom held a prominent place in British mythology is certain from the allusions made to it by the bards. Taliesin, in the description of this initiation into the mysteries of the basin, cries out, 'I have lost my speech!' because on all who had been admitted to the privileges of full membership secrecy was imposed. This initiation was regarded as a new birth; and those who had once become joined members were regarded as elect, regenerate, separate from the rest of mankind, who lay in darkness and ignorance.

That originally the ceremonies of initiation included human sacrifices is more than probable from the vessel being represented as containing human blood, and a lance forming part of the paraphernalia, from which dropped blood. In the story of Pheredur, the vessel contained a man's head floating in gore. In that of Bran the Blessed, the head is thrown into the basin to destroy its efficacy. Taliesin also refers to Pheredur as 'the hero of the bleeding head.'

The lance is also referred to by Welsh authors. One of the predictions attributed to Taliesin holds out to the Britons the hope that 'the Kingdom of Logres (England) shall perish before the bleeding lance'; and five centuries later, Chrétien de Troyes quotes this saying –

> Il est écrit qu'il est une heure,
> Où tout le royaume de Logres,
> Qui jadis fut la terre ès Ogres,
> Sera détruit par cette lance.

This lance was probably a symbol of war.

The first to adapt the druidic mystery to Christianity was a British hermit, who wrote a Latin legend on the subject. Helinandus (d. 1227) says, 'At this time (A.D. 720), in Britain, a marvellous vision was shown by an angel to a certain hermit: it was of the basin or paropsis in which the Saviour supped with His disciples; concerning which the history was written by the same hermit, which is called the Gradal.' And he adds, 'In French they give the name gradal, or graal, to a large, rather deep vessel, in which rich meats with their gravy are served to the wealthy.'

The date at which lived this anchorite is not certain, for though Helinandus says he had his vision in 720, Usher places him later than 1140.

After the composition of this legend, the romancers took possession of the myth and adapted it to Christian chivalrous exigencies. The bardic table of the elect became the round-table of Arthur's knights, and the sacred vessel of mysteries became the Grail. The head of the victim was forgotten, and the sacrificial blood was supposed to be that of Christ.

It is likely that the tradition of the ancient druidic brotherhood lingered on and gained consistency again among the Templars. Just as the Miles Templi fought for the holy sepulchre, so did the soldier of Montsalvatsch for the holy Grail. Both orders were vowed to chastity and obedience, both were subject to a head, who exercised regal authority. The ancient temple of the Grail, like Stonehenge, was circular; so also were the churches dedicated to S. Sepulchre, by the soldier monks. The charge of heresy was brought against the order of the Templars, and it has been supposed that they were imbued with gnosticism. That this Eastern heresy should have influenced a mediæval Western society, I think very unlikely; no other traces of gnosticism are to be found in the religious history of the Occident, which certainly would have been the case had the heresy been sufficiently powerful to have obtained mastery over an ecclesiastical society. I think the root of the false doctrine or practices of the Templars must be looked for in the West.

The Templars were charged with having an idol which the Chronicles of S. Denys (which terminate 1461) describe as 'an old skin embalmed and polished, in which the Templar places his very vile faith and trust, and in which he confidently believes: and it has in the sockets eyes of carbuncle shining with the brightness of the sky.'

Abraham Bzov, in his continuation of the 'Church History' of Baronius, quotes a charge brought by the Italian bishops against the Templars, to this effect: 'They have a certain head, the face pale like that of a man, with black curled hair, and round the neck a gilded ornament, which indeed belonged to no saint, and this they adored, making prayers before it.' And one of the questions asked by the Pope of the witnesses was, 'whether they had not a skull or some sort of image, to which they rendered divine homage?' So also the Chronicle of Meaux states, that on the first day of the General Council of the Templars, a head with a white beard, which had belonged to a former Grand Master of the Order, was set at midnight before the altar in a chapel, covered with silken robes and precious stuffs. Mass was sung before daylight, and the head was then adored by the Master and the other knights.

It seems to me probable that this head, if there were truth in the charge, was revered because it was part of an ancient druidic rite to produce a head upon a vessel, though for what purposes we do not know. Friar Bacon constructed a head which gave oracles. Possibly some such property was attributed to the Templar, and previously to the druidic head. Livy tells us that a bloody head of an enemy was a national Keltic symbol, and that the Boii brought the head into their temples, where they cleansed it and adorned it with gold, and then used it on festivals for a sacred vessel, out of which to make drink-offerings.

To enter with any thing like completeness into the most interesting and intricate subject of druidic mythology and ceremonial would occupy too much space. This paper will necessarily be imperfect; the religion of our British ancestors has yet to be written. Those who have hitherto approached the subject have so done with preconceived theories which have caused them to read wrong the sacred myths and rites they were interpreting. Much is to be learned from the Arthurian Romances, much from bardic remains, and much from Breton, Welsh, Gaelic, and Irish folk-lore.

That all thus recovered will be in a corrupted form I am well aware, but a practised eye will be able to restore what is disintegrated, and will know to detect antiquity, though disguised under the newest robe.

A careful study of these sources, conducted by the light of comparative mythology, will, I am satisfied, lead to the discovery that, under the name of Methodism, we have the old druidic religion still alive, energetic, and possibly more vigorous than it was when it exercised a spiritual supremacy over the whole of Britain. With the loss of the British tongue, much of the old terminology has died out, and a series of adaptations to Christianity has taken place, without radically affecting the system.

Further Reading

Chapter 1 Prester John

Beckingham, C. F., *The Achievements of Prester John* (London: University of London, 1966).

Gumilev, L. N., *Searches for An Imaginary Kingdom*, translated by R. E. F. Smith (Cambridge: Cambridge University Press, 1987).

Slessarev, Vsevolod, *Prester John: The Letter and the Legend* (Minneapolis: University of Minnesota Press, 1959).

Ullendorff, Edward and C. F. Beckingham, *The Hebrew Letters of Prester John* (Oxford: Oxford University Press, 1982).

Chapter 2 The Seven Sleepers of Ephesus

Hole, Christina, *English Folk Heroes* (London: Batsford, 1948).

Jobes, Gertrude, *Dictionary of Mythology, Folklore and Symbols* (New York: Scarecrow Press, 1961).

Matthews, Caitlin, 'The Guardian Head', in *The Aquarian Guide to Legendary London* edited by John Matthews and Chesca Potter (Wellingborough: Aquarian Press, 1990).

Chapter 3 The Dog Gellert

Gantz, Jeffrey, *The Mabinogion* (Harmondsworth: Penguin Books, 1976).

Gwyndaf, Robin, *Welsh Folk Tales* (Cardiff: National Museum of Wales, 1989).

Matthews, John, 'Arthur and Gorlagon', in *The Unknown Arthur: Forgotten Tales of the Round Table* (London: Blandford Press, 1995).

Nizami, Ganjavi, *The Story of Layla and Majnun* (Oxford: Bruno Cassimer, 1966).

Chapter 4 Antichrist and Pope Joan

Douglas, Alfred, *The Tarot* (Harmondsworth: Penguin Books, 1973).

Durrell, Lawrence, *Pope Joan*, translated and adapted from the Greek of Emmanuel Royidis (London: Peter Owen, 1981).

Forsyth, Neil, *The Old Enemy: Satan and the Combat Myth* (Princeton, NJ: Princeton University Press, 1987).

Metford, J. C. J., *Dictionary of Christian Lore and Legend* (London: Thames & Hudson, 1983).

Stoyanov, Yuri, *Hidden Tradition in Europe* (London: Penguin Books Arkana, 1994).

Chapter 5   The Man in the Moon

Biedermann, Hans, *Dictionary of Symbolism* (New York: Penguin Books, 1994).

McCrickard, Janet, *Eclipse of the Sun: An Investigation into Sun and Moon Myths* (Glastonbury: Gothic Image Publications, 1990).

Plutarch, 'Concerning the Face which Appears in the Orb of the Moon', translated by Harold Cherniss, in *Moralia*, vol. XII (London: Heinemann; Cambridge, MA: Harvard University Press, 1957).

Riordan, James, *The Woman in the Moon and Other Stories of Forgotten Heroines* (London: Hutchinson, 1984).

Tolkien, J. R. R., *The Lord of the Rings* (London: George Allen & Unwin, 1954–5).

Chapter 6   The Mountain of Venus

Anon, 'The Chymical Wedding of Christian Rosencreutz', in *A Christian Rosenkreutz Anthology*, edited by Paul M. Allen (New York: Rudolf Steiner Publications, 1968).

Barto, Philip Stephan, *Tannhäuser and the Mountain of Venus* (New York: Oxford University Press, 1916).

Mann, Thomas, *The Magic Mountain* (London: Penguin Books, 1962).

Matthews, Caitlín, 'The Rosicrucian Vault as Sepulchre and Wedding Chamber', in *The Underworld Initiation* by R. J. Stewart (Wellingborough: Aquarian Press, 1985).

Newman, Ernest, *The Wagner Operas* (New York: Knopf, 1949).

Chapter 7   The Terrestrial Paradise

Giamatti, A. B., *The Earthly Paradise and the Renaissance Epic* (Princeton, NJ: Princeton University Press, 1966).

Heinberg, Richard, *Memories and Visions of Paradise* (Wellingborough: Thorsons, 1990).

Levin, Harry, *The Myth of the Golden Age in the Renaissance* (Bloomington, IN: University of Indiana Press, 1969).

Matthews, Caitlín, *The Celtic Book of the Dead: A Guide for Your Voyage to the Celtic Otherworld* (London: Aquarian Press, 1992).

——, 'The Quest as Shamanic Journey', in *The Encyclopedia of Celtic Wisdom* by John and Caitlín Matthews (Shaftesbury, Dorset: Element Books, 1994).

Chapter 8   Melusine

Duggan, Alfred, *The Devil's Brood: The Angevin Family* (London: Faber and Faber, 1957).

Gwyndaff, Robin, *Welsh Folk Tales* (Cardiff: National Museum of Wales, 1989).

Keightley, Thomas, *The Fairy Mythology* (London: Wildwood House, 1981).

Lainez, Manuel Mujica, *The Wandering Unicorn* (London: Chatto & Windus, 1983).

Chapter 9   The Fortunate Isles

Geoffrey of Monmouth, *The* Vita Merlini (*The Life of Merlin*) by John Jay Parry (Urbana, IL: University of Illinois, 1925).

Loffler, Christa Maria, *The Voyage to the Otherworld Island in Early Irish Literature* 2 vols (Salzburg: Institut für Anglistik und Amerikanistik Universität Salzburg, 1983).

McGlone, William C. and P. M. Leonard, *Ancient Celtic America* (Fresno, CA: Panorama West Books, 1986).

Sinclair, Andrew, *The Sword and the Grail: Of the Grail and the Templars and a True Discovery of America* (New York: Crown, 1992).

Chapter 10   Swan-Maidens

Biedermann, Hans, *Dictionary of Symbolism* (New York: Penguin Books, 1994).

Green, Miranda, *Animals in Celtic Life and Myth* (London: Routledge, 1992).

Jobes, Gertrude, *Dictionary of Mythology, Folklore and Symbols* (New York: Scarecrow Press, 1961).

Matthews, John, 'Guingamore and Gueherres', in *The Unknown Arthur: Forgotten Tales of the Round Table* (London: Blandford Press, 1995).

Chapter 11   The Knight of the Swan

Dopp, Herman, 'Le Chevalier au Cygne et Godefroid de Bouillon', in *Bulletin of the Faculty of Arts*, Fouad University, III, 1935, pp. 148–62.

Frey, Anna Louise, *The Swan-Knight Legend, its Background, Early Development, and Treatment in the German Poems* (Nashville: George Peabody College for Teachers, 1931).

Jaffray, Robert, *The Two Knights of the Swan, Lohengrin and Helyas* (New York and London: G. P. Putnam, 1910).

Chapter 12   The Sangreal

Chrétien de Troyes, *Perceval, or the Story of the Grail*, trans. by W. W. Kliber, in *Arthurian Romances* (London: Penguin Books, 1991).

Currer-Briggs, Noel, *The Shroud and the Grail* (London: Weidenfeld & Nicolson, 1987).

Lacy, Norris, et al. (ed. and trans.), *The Lancelot-Grail* 5 vols (London and New York: Garland, 1993–6).

Matthews, John, *The Grail: Quest for the Eternal* (London: Thames & Hudson, 1981).

——, *Elements of the Grail Tradition* (Shaftesbury, Dorset: Element Books, 1991).

——, *King Arthur and the Grail* (London: Blandford Press, 1994).

Index